# TRAUMA-SENSITIVE SCHOOLS for the ADOLESCENT YEARS

# TRAUMA-SENSITIVE SCHOOLS for the ADOLESCENT YEARS
## Promoting Resiliency and Healing, Grades 6–12

Susan E. Craig

Foreword by Jim Sporleder

**TEACHERS COLLEGE PRESS**

**TEACHERS COLLEGE** | COLUMBIA UNIVERSITY
NEW YORK AND LONDON

Published by Teachers College Press, 1234 Amsterdam Avenue, New York, NY 10027

Copyright © 2017 by Teachers College, Columbia University

Cover photo by Nika Fadul, Getty Images.

Figure 2.2 "Original ACE Pyramid" reprinted with permission from Vincent Felitti, MD.

Figure 2.3 Expanded ACE Pyramid is reprinted with permission of Kanwarpal Dhaliwal and was adapted by RYSE Center © 2016.

*Library of Congress Cataloging-in-Publication Data*

Names: Craig, Susan E., author.
Title: Trauma-sensitive schools for the adolescent years : promoting
    resiliency and healing, grades 6-12 / Susan E. Craig ; foreword by Jim
    Sporleder.
Description: New York, NY : Teachers College Press, 2017. | Includes
    bibliographical references and index.
Identifiers: LCCN 2017024039| ISBN 9780807758250 (pbk. : alk. paper) | ISBN
    9780807776513 (ebook)
Subjects: LCSH: Children with mental disabilities–Education (Secondary) |
    Psychic trauma in children. | Post-traumatic stress disorder in children.
    | Educational psychology. | Community and school. | Teacher-student
    relationships.
Classification: LCC LC4604 .C73 2017 | DDC 371.92/8–dc23

LC record available at https://lccn.loc.gov/2017024039
ISBN 978-0-8077-5825-0 (paper)
ISBN 978-0-8077-7651-3 (ebook)

Printed on acid-free paper
Manufactured in the United States of America

24  23  22  21  20  19  18  17        8  7  6  5  4  3  2  1

# Contents

# Foreword

Public schools are at a critical crossroads. They face challenges on all sides: legislative mandates and educational policy written by legislators who have never been in a classroom; negative public opinion ratings; a growing number of students with behavior problems who are unprepared for and disconnected from the learning environment; and despite great effort, only minor improvements in student performance. As a result, the stress level is high for adults working in schools. Some of our best teachers leave the profession because they are unable to cope with their own "burnout" and sense of hopelessness.

As a principal of the first public high school in the country to adopt a trauma-informed and resiliency-building approach, I know it is possible to change our approach and make a difference. At the Lincoln Alternative High School in Walla Walla, WA, when we embraced a trauma-informed approach in 2011, miracles began to happen. As teachers learned to appreciate the effects of toxic stress on learning rather than to simply react to students' behavior, the school suspension rate decreased by 85%. Not long after, Lincoln High School started getting the results staff thought were out of our reach only months before: higher attendance, higher grade point averages, higher graduation rates, and fewer discipline problems. *Trauma-Sensitive Schools for the Adolescent Years: Promoting Resiliency and Healing, Grades 6–12* provides schools with the guidance they need to have the kind of turn around we saw in Walla Walla, and embark on the path of implementing "trauma sensitive schools."

Dr. Susan Craig lays out a sequential plan for implementation of the trauma-sensitive school. She clearly provides the neuroscience on how trauma has a direct correlation with a child's brain development, and how this impacts her or his behavior. As Heather T. Forbes, LCSW, and author of *Help for Billy* shares, "we don't have a behavior issue, we have a brain issue." The students that have been impacted by toxic home environments (as well as additional toxicity from their larger community) develop a brain for survival. The survival brain is not a bad brain, but it is a brain that is always on alert, due to the unpredictability and harm caused by environments in which adolescents have very little or no agency. As you will learn from this book, it is the caregivers of these children that are responsible for their brain development, and we know that the brain drives the students' behavior. If we take a moment to reflect, we will see how the author connects the dots for us and explains why we are seeing more and more students coming to us unprepared, and why we are dealing with such challenging behavior. When we look at how pervasive these traumatic experiences are, and how they pile up, we gain a deeper understanding as to the significant effect of trauma on students in our middle and secondary schools.

There is compelling evidence-based research to support a trauma-informed approach to student discipline. Susan Craig's book provides the scientific evidence and the reasons why it is so critical that schools take this new path in serving our students. The trauma-sensitive school approach is "best practice" for all students, and it will bring about the changes we want to see for everyone. Why? Because we know that a trauma-informed approach is the pathway to providing a "safe haven" where our struggling students acquire the resilience they need in a safe school environment; an environment where the adults intentionally develop caring adult relationships with all of their students. Morally, this is what every one of our students deserves: a pathway to becoming the person they were meant to be, not how they are defined by their negative toxic environment. You can choose the path to becoming a trauma-sensitive school with confidence. The neuroscience is clear: healthy caring adult relationships teach resilience, which leads to changing students' negative belief systems, which then opens the door to hope, healing, and optimism for their future.

I believe that it is paramount for us to use this evidence-based research to guide us in this most rewarding journey. Hurting kids can grow up to become hurting adults who hurt others. A school that employees a trauma-sensitive "lens" to care for their students has the powerful opportunity to help a hurting student become a resilient and confident adult capable of breaking through the barriers of trauma. Students then have the resilience to use their experiences as stepping-stones for personal growth and to become contributing members of our society. As educators, this is the most priceless gift we have to offer our students impacted by trauma. We can't reach 100% of our students, but we can love them 100%.

I think you will find this book a valuable guide on your journey to becoming a trauma-sensitive school. And you will find that as you work to transform your students, they will transform you. A trauma-sensitive school isn't what you do, it becomes who you are as a school culture, and your motivation to create the one caring adult relationship that can influence your students' paths in becoming the people that each of them is meant to be.

–Jim Sporleder, retired principal
Lincoln Alternative High School, Walla Walla, WA,
profiled in the documentary film "Paper Tigers" and
coauthor, with Heather T. Forbes, *The Trauma-Informed School:*
*A Step-by-Step Implementation Guide for Administrators and School Personnel*

# Introduction

My interest in understanding the relationships between violence and children's cognitive development began in the early 1980s when I was working as a reading teacher. I wanted to know why so many young, aggressive children, who did not meet the criteria for learning disabilities or mental retardation, were unable to read. The question led me to doctoral studies at the University of New Hampshire's Family Research Lab, where I completed a dissertation on the effects of violence on children's cognitive development. The results showed a relationship between exposure to family violence and deficits in children's language development, memory, attention, and locus of control. Concerns about the causal direction of the relationships tempered the power of these findings.

Disagreements about causality were still an issue in 1992 when I published the article "The Educational Needs of Children Living in Violence" in *Phi Delta Kappan.* Some argued that abuse and neglect caused the observed developmental anomalies (Money, 1982). Others favored the view that children with developmental disabilities were more difficult to nurture, thus increasing their risk of maltreatment (Martin, 1979).

Since then, retrospective studies (Felitti et al., 1998) and research on children's neurological development (National Scientific Council on the Developing Child 2005, 2006, 2007, 2012) have resolved these issues. There is no longer any doubt that violence and chronic exposure to toxic stress disrupt the process of normal child development (Perkins & Graham-Bermann, 2012). These experiences alter the architecture of children's brains in ways that threaten their ability to achieve academic and social competence. Left unattended, these changes can put children on a trajectory of increasingly challenging behaviors and disengagement from school. Once they become teen-agers, their victimization often continues at home, in the community, and at school. Coupled with the developmental challenges of adolescence, unresolved or ongoing trauma leaves teens without the resources they need to create purpose and meaning in their lives.

*Trauma-Sensitive Schools for the Adolescent Years: Promoting Resiliency and Healing, Grades 6–12* offers teachers and administrators guidance in knowing how to recognize the symptoms of trauma. Using strategies that can be integrated into the daily lives of schools, practitioners are able to mitigate trauma's devastating consequences and offer hope to the students in their care.

The continued high prevalence of trauma in children's lives suggests that trauma is a common pathway to academic and social problems. Teachers need to recognize the symptoms of early trauma and know how to intervene in ways that mitigate its devastating consequences. *Trauma-Sensitive Schools for the Adolescent Years: Promoting Resiliency and Healing, Grades 6–12* provides readers with an overview of what they need to know about trauma, as well as strategies to create and sustain a trauma-sensitive environment.

## THE ADOLESCENT BRAIN

Adolescence is a period of rapid neural development. It is a critical period for everyone, but particularly so for children with trauma histories. It is a time that lends itself well to repairing dysfunctional adaptations as a result of early stress. The brain is especially malleable during this period. Developmentally appropriate, supportive environments help adolescents benefit from this remarkably high level of neuroplasticity by strengthening the neural pathways connecting the reptilian brain to the cerebral cortex. This improved circuitry increases teenagers' capacity for self-regulation, executive functioning, and problem solving (Siegel, 2013a; Steinberg, 2014).

Unfortunately, pervasive misunderstanding of adolescent development and ill-informed policies aimed at punishing rather than repairing juvenile misbehaviors limit the advantages that could be derived from appropriately guiding youth's neural development during this critical period. Despite a growing body of research that challenges traditional assumptions about how to improve the academic and social mastery of failing teens, middle and secondary schools—especially those in urban areas—continue to view students' underperformance as an intentional disregard for learning and discipline. With little or no training in how to recognize or repair the effects of unresolved trauma on adolescent behavior, staff members attempt to increase interest and cooperation using a combination of high expectations, strictly enforced rules, and severe consequences for noncompliance. The results? A dropout rate approaching 50% in urban areas and an alarming "school-to-prison pipeline" that criminalizes behaviors such as talking back to a teacher or violating the school dress code (Heilzeg, 2009).

No amount of goodwill alone can resolve these issues. Improving adolescent academic achievement and social mastery requires a commitment to integrating knowledge of the effects of trauma on adolescent development into efforts at educational reform. Historically, this has not been the case. Neither No Child Left Behind (NCLB) nor Race to the Top includes research or information developed outside an educational framework. Neither is influenced by the wealth of neuroscience research that is available on the developing brain and its effects on learning and behavior (Caine & Caine, 1990; Jensen, 2008; Willis, 2007). As a result, readily available explanations of the relationship between early adversity, neural development, and school success fail to have the impact they should on issues of school climate, discipline, or instructional best practices in secondary schools.

*Trauma-Sensitive Schools for the Adolescent Years* encourages readers to view future efforts at school improvement through a trauma-sensitive lens—a lens that will help school personnel understand what trauma is, recognize its detrimental effects on development, and appreciate the pervasiveness of its symptoms. Only then can educators and policymakers promote reforms that foster resiliency and make the necessary changes that will improve students' academic and social mastery.

## DESIGN OF THE BOOK

Chapter 1, Trauma-Sensitive Secondary Schools, provides an overview of the history of the trauma-sensitive school movement and the role it plays in reversing the failure of recent zero-tolerance or exclusionary discipline policies. It suggests that trauma-sensitive secondary schools represent a new vision for promoting adolescent resilience. A detailed description of the assumptions and components of the trauma-sensitive school model is presented.

Chapter 2, Addressing the Many Faces of Adolescent Trauma, explores the prevalence of adolescent trauma and its effects on neurodevelopment. The traumatic effects of marginalization on adolescent functioning are presented, particularly in terms of minority populations. This chapter explains how participation in inclusive school communities can help teens overcome these difficulties.

Chapter 3, Remodeling the Adolescent Brain for Adulthood, describes the neurological changes that take place in adolescence, with an emphasis on those occurring in the cerebral cortex. How these changes affect adolescents' executive functioning, social cognition, and capacity for abstract thought is discussed, as well as the variations in performance that can occur as a result of trauma. Threats to successful remodeling are presented, including mental illness, social isolation, and suicidal ideation.

Chapter 4, Re-Traumatization on the Streets, sheds light on the prevalence of community violence in the lives of adolescents. Common types of adolescent victimization are identified with suggested trauma-informed responses that can be implemented in schools. The relationship between trauma and delinquency is explored, as well as how zero-tolerance discipline policies contribute to the problem. The chapter ends with a discussion of the high prevalence of substance abuse among teens with trauma histories, and the devastating effects it can have on them.

Chapter 5, The Neurobiology of Interdependence, discusses the effects of trauma on attachment and self-individuation. The role attachment plays in adolescent behavior and social interdependence is explored. Various models of adult attachment are described, as well as the support that teens with trauma histories need to achieve secure attachments as adults.

Chapter 6, The Teacher's Role in Trauma-Sensitive Schools, begins with a discussion of adolescent neurodevelopment and instructional best practices. The benefits of differentiated instruction and dialogic teaching are reviewed, including the contributions each can make to teens' developing sense of self-efficacy and self-awareness. A system of tiered intervention is proposed as well as strategies teachers can use to create collaborative partnerships with students.

Chapter 7, Trauma and Resilience, targets directions schools can take to foster resilience among adolescents exposed to trauma. The need to establish a culture of connection is discussed, as well as strategies for promoting positive peer interactions and collective efficacy. Strategies schools can use to help teens develop optimism and take an active role in their own well-being are presented.

Chapter 8, The Effects of Secondary Trauma on Teachers' Lives, explores the emotional toll of working with traumatized teens and its possible relationship to teacher attrition. The need for training that informs teachers about the contagious nature of trauma is discussed in addition to ways of promoting teacher resilience.

Chapter 9, Next Steps: Managing the Necessary Changes to School Policies and Practices, provides an overview of steps to consider as schools adopt a trauma-sensitive approach. These include an awareness of the complexity of the proposed changes, as well as the resources required to sustain enthusiasm and support for the process. The role of district and local leadership is discussed, in addition to the need for progress monitoring and evaluation of student outcomes.

## CONCLUSION

Though one book cannot resolve all the issues related to trauma and learning, it can raise awareness of a problem that threatens the viability of a valued resource—America's public schools. The path to true school reform requires educators to embrace the insights neuroscience provides into this troubling barrier to adolescents' academic and social competence. The goal of writing *Trauma-Sensitive Schools for the Adolescent Years* is to provide educators with guidance along the way.

# CHAPTER 1

# Trauma-Sensitive Secondary Schools

> You don't need permission from other people to make your school a better place.
>
> —Richard Dufour

By definition, trauma-sensitive schools are safe zones, which buffer students from external forces that threaten their potential, while at the same time fostering the skills teens need to regulate internal emotions and drives. Staff members in trauma-sensitive middle and secondary schools are attuned to the risks and opportunities that characterize adolescent development. They know that teenagers are three times more likely than younger children to suffer multiple victimizations by multiple perpetrators (Finkelhor, Turner, Hamby, & Ormrod, 2011). Especially vulnerable are those marginalized by race, sexual orientation, disability, poverty, or immigration status.

This chapter discusses the historical evolution of the trauma-sensitive schools movement as a response to failed zero-tolerance policies, and the growing awareness of the role that trauma plays in adolescents' school engagement and neural development. An explanation of the assumptions of the model is provided, as well as a review of its component parts. Together, these provide a viable framework to respond to the high prevalence of trauma among students in secondary schools.

## THE IMPORTANCE OF THE TRAUMA-SENSITIVE SCHOOLS MOVEMENT

The trauma-sensitive schools movement is the result of a confluence of forces that are changing the paradigm through which educators view the academic and social problems faced by students. First among these is the failure of exclusionary discipline policies to create safe schools and improve academic and social outcomes for teens. This failure's occurring in the 1990s, "the Decade of the Brain" (a term used by President George H. W. Bush to increase public awareness of the advances being made in neuroscience) was ironic. As evidence emerged to suggest a relationship between trauma and neural development in adolescence, schools were challenged take a new look at how trauma affects student learning. Studies linking trauma to low student engagement as indicated by high absenteeism (Balfanz & Byrnes, 2012), poor academic performance, and high dropout rates (Porche, Fortuna, Lin, & Alegria, 2011) led educators to realize the need for a new vision for promoting adolescent resilience and success–the vision of a trauma-sensitive school.

## Failure of Exclusionary Discipline

In the period following the Columbine High School shootings in 1999, schools embraced zero-tolerance discipline policies aimed at keeping schools safe. These policies impose severe penalties on students without regard for individual circumstances. Since that tumultuous time, boundaries between school and police authority have often been blurred, with many schools relying on law enforcement to handle minor misconduct (Elais, 2013).

Almost 20 years later, it is clear that rather than improving school safety, zero-tolerance policies put students at increased risk of arrest for being tardy, showing defiance for school rules, or disturbing the peace. In many states, there continues to be a tendency to view prison as the default educational placement for children whose behavior is deemed unruly or out of control (Nance, 2015). Adolescents of color and those with emotional disabilities are disproportionally represented in this so-called "school-to-prison pipeline" (Quinn, Rutherford, & Leone, 2001; Snyder, 2005). Despite efforts on the part of the American Bar Association (ABA Juvenile Justice Committee, 2001), civil rights organizations such as the Southern Poverty Law Center, the U.S. Senate (Senator Dick Durbin, D-Illinois, 2012), and the NEA (Flannery, 2015), zero-tolerance policies remain an ongoing threat to youth's ability to access a free and appropriate public school education. Trauma-sensitive schools offer an alternative to this type of exclusionary discipline.

## Growing Evidence of the Relationship Between Trauma and Low Student Engagement

Disconnected youth are frequently tardy or absent, and often receive poor or failing grades. When they do come to school, they often engage in disruptive behavior that can disturb their own learning as well as that of peers. Traditional explanations for these behaviors often emphasize their volitional aspects, suggesting that they occur as a result of bad choices or intentional defiance. Recommended interventions are contingency-based, suggesting that all teens will work for the right reward, or to avoid negative consequences. The inability of these techniques to effect desired changes in student behavior leaves many teachers struggling to understand why.

Recent studies of trauma and self-regulation provide an explanation (Siegel, 2012). Throughout life, a person's interpretation of danger involves a dialogue between the subcortical brain, immediately below the cerebral cortex, and the more sophisticated cortex. The cerebral cortex is the site of consciousness and higher-order thinking. It is the outer layer of the brain and is made up of folded gray matter (see Figure 1.1).

Early trauma limits adolescents' ability to use higher-order thinking to regulate subcortical brain activity. Their thinking is "held hostage" by relentless fear and hyperarousal that derail focus needed to achieve academically. Frustrated, teens with trauma histories often disengage from school. The dropout rate among the 38% of adolescents reporting traumatic experiences prior to age 16 is close to 20%, a rate significantly higher than that of adolescents who do not report a history of trauma (Porche, Fortuna, Lin, & Alegria, 2011).

Staff members in trauma-sensitive schools recognize the frustration and hopelessness that motivates traumatized students, and they take active steps to help students address these feelings. The first step is to acknowledge that the academic challenges students face seem overwhelming, and that the thought of addressing them triggers a "fight, flight, or freeze" response (Hammond, 2015). This acknowledgment validates teens' experience and serves as an invitation to explore the idea of collaborating with teachers to address an agreed-upon learning goal. Hammond (2015) describes the ensuing teacher–student relationship as similar to the therapeutic alliance

## Figure 1.1. The Human Brain

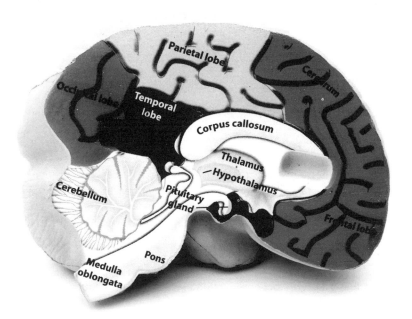

forged between therapists and clients. The teacher serves as a coregulator of students' emotional response to the learning process in a manner that encourages continued engagement and progress toward the agreed-upon goal. As teens become more confident in both their skills and their ability to regulate their emotions, engagement in both learning and the larger school community improves.

## The Effects of Systemic Devaluation and Unresolved Trauma on Neural Development

As children grow into adolescence, their chance of exposure to prejudice and discrimination on the basis of collective identity (race, ethnicity, socio-economic status, gender identity, religion) goes up (Smith-Bynum, Lambert, English, & Ialongo, 2014). This often exacerbates the effects of earlier trauma and inhibits efforts at recovery (Kira, 2010). Youth of color are disproportionally at risk for experiencing an additional set of traumatizing events as a result of race-based inequities (Carter, 2007). This is due in part to the way social institutions, including schools, judge their behavior.

Traditionally, Western cultures view children as more innocent and more in need of protection than adults (Haslam, Rothschild, & Ernst, 2000). The perceived innocence of Black children, however, is more short-lived than that of their White peers. By age 10, the perceived innocence of Black children is equivalent to that of much older White children. By adolescence, Black boys ages 14 to 17 are perceived as bringing the same level of culpability for their behavior as White boys ages 18 to 21 (Goff, Jackson, DiLeone, Culotta, & DiTomasso, 2014). Some studies suggest that Black children may be viewed as adults as early as age 13 (Kimmel, 2008). This perception of Black children as more responsible for their behavior than White children of the same age reduces the protections given to them. They are seen as less innocent than their peers, and, therefore, more vulnerable to harsh, adult-like consequences.

By definition, trauma involves exposure to experiences that exceed one's capacity to cope (Corcoran & Roberts, 2015). It is, therefore, not difficult to imagine the incredible stress involved in being held to a level of performance and accountability that exceeds the developmental expectations of one's age. This is especially true when the failure to live up to these unrealistic expectations is labeled as proof of a poor attitude and judged worthy of disciplinary action. As a result, the already-compromised sense of personal agency and self-worth shared by victims of early trauma is further reduced threatening students' ability to  increase neural connectivity—myelination and executive functioning (Siegel, 2013a).

*Reclaiming Lost Innocence.* Trauma-sensitive approaches to educating adolescents begin with replacing harsh judgments of their misdeeds with curiosity about why the misdeeds are occurring. The goal is to replace past experiences of insufficient protection and support from caregivers with a proactive willingness to help. This serves to increase students' understanding of the negative relationship between trauma and the reactive behaviors it spawns. Only then can they begin to address the emotional dysregulation, social processing errors, and persistent problems with aggression that limit their ability to achieve academic and social mastery. A willingness to wonder "What happened to you?" or "What did others do to you?" helps staff in trauma-sensitive schools create the environment that youth need to move beyond past trauma and prevent concurrent trauma.

*Strengthening Neural Pathways.* Adolescence represents a second window of opportunity in brain development. It is a period when increases in neural connectivity facilitate the development of improved communication between the subcortical brain and the more sophisticated cortex. The cerebral cortex is the site of consciousness and higher-order thinking. Experiences during adolescence that encourage its development help teens exert control over the impulsivity and dysregulation caused by early trauma (Ahmed, Bittencourt-Hewitt, & Sebastian 2015). They are able to "put the brakes" on the reactive subcortical brain long enough to evaluate a situation and decide on a reasonable course of action.

The instructional strategies that are most beneficial to traumatized adolescents are those that promote the integration of new information into existing knowledge, while fostering collaboration with peers and improved perspective taking. When used consistently, these interventions help teens acquire insight into their own thoughts and behavior, while developing empathy for others. They learn to make use of past experiences and project the implications of current behaviors on future outcomes.

## A NEW VISION FOR PROMOTING ADOLESCENT RESILIENCE

The risk of trauma exposure increases dramatically among adolescents (Ruzek, Brymer, Jacobs, Layne, Vernberg, & Watson, 2007). By age 18, 43% of youth have experienced a traumatic event. This means that over a third of the students in middle school and high school are struggling to manage the effects of trauma and victimization. Within the population with trauma histories, some experience multiple types of adversity, thereby increasing their behavioral symptoms and impairment in adolescence (Finkelhor, Ormrod, & Turner, 2007). Others are managing the residual effects of early traumas that are still unresolved. In either case, energy that should be going into learning and exploration is instead being directed toward vigilance and self-protective adaptations. As a result, neural pathways leading to rapid, automatic adjustments to prevent harm or decrease arousal are activated frequently, while neurons involved in complex learning and adaptation are dormant. This poses problems for brain development during adolescence, a period of extensive neural pruning. Habitually activated neural connections become stronger, while inactive neurons die off (Belsky & de Hann, 2011). In other words, because of the use-dependent nature of the brain, repeated firing of stress-activated neurons rather than those associated with higher-order thinking, threatens the development of the complex neural networks needed to accomplish the developmental tasks of adolescence and adulthood (Cicchetti, 2006).

Because the stakes are so high, schools can no longer afford to ignore the high prevalence of trauma in the student population. Fortunately, more states are recognizing trauma as a public health epidemic and developing ways to mitigate its devastating effects. In 2005 Massachusetts was first to coin the phrase *trauma-sensitive schools* to describe the school climate, instructional designs, positive behavioral supports, and policies needed to help traumatized students achieve academic and social competence. Since then, trauma-sensitive schools have opened in California (2009), Pennsylvania (2011), Washington (2010), and Wisconsin (2010). These are among the states that continue to lead the effort to draw national attention to the prevalence of trauma among children and adolescents. Additionally, these states recognize the need to include the creation of trauma-sensitive environments in future efforts at educational reform. Evidence of the momentum for trauma-sensitive reform is apparent in the fact that the Every Student Succeeds Act (ESSA) signed by President Obama on December 10, 2015, includes many provisions that qualify as "trauma-informed," such as those to reduce over-testing and overuse of exclusionary discipline practices as well as those that recognize the importance of early learning. There also are notable provisions that secure a specific foothold for "trauma-informed practices." Among these are grants to fund "high-quality support for school personnel, including specialized instructional support personnel" for effective and trauma-informed practices in classroom management, along with support for other programs such as suicide prevention, crisis management and conflict resolution techniques, and human trafficking prevention" (Sec. 4108(5)(A)(ii); (D)).

## Assumptions of Trauma-Sensitive Secondary Schools

Adolescence marks the transition from childhood innocence to adult responsibility. It is a time of life characterized by increased emotional intensity and a high need for social engagement (Siegel, 2013a). Students whose early lives were spent in secure, safe environments enter this transitional period with confidence knowing they have the ability to regulate their emotions, adjust to changing expectations of their behavior, and achieve their goals. They are able to connect with others as a source of nourishment and strength.

Students whose first relationships fail to provide them with the care and protection they need develop survival strategies to cope with their feelings of disconnection, dysregulation, disorganization, and isolation. When they reach adolescence, these early adaption or survival strategies can have a profoundly negative impact on their neural development, their capacity to form relationships, and their ability to succeed at school.

Establishing a link between childhood adversity and subsequent adolescent conduct places the origin of maladaptive behaviors within an interpersonal context. In this model, challenging attitudes or modes of comportment are seen as a direct or indirect result of an "injury," often inflicted by a caregiver. These injuries include physical, emotional, and social maltreatment, which affect the social interactivity required for healthy brain development. Deprived of needed care and protection, children develop a series of biological adaptations that change the way the brain, the neuroendocrine stress response, and the immune system function, both individually and cooperatively (Johnson, Riley, Granger, & Riis, 2013). These adaptions are essential for children's survival, but they create serious long-term limitations on children's ability to cope with the academic and social demands of school.

## Components of the Model

The trauma-sensitive framework is flexible, meaning it can be personalized to meet the needs of local school communities (Cole, Eisner, Gregory, & Ristuccia, 2013). There are, however, several model components that facilitate the implementation of a trauma-sensitive approach.

*Staff Training and Supervision.* Teachers and school administrators are trained to view existing supports and interventions through a trauma-sensitive lens. Professional development is provided on the sensory nature of unresolved trauma and how to make accommodations that are responsive to the challenges this presents. Close collaboration with neighborhood mental health agencies ensures the availability of additional resources for students in crisis or whose needs require short-term targeted interventions (Craig, 2008). Trauma-sensitive supervision helps teachers maintain positive relationships with students and avoid falling prey to compassion fatigue or vicarious traumatization (Figley, 2002).

*Instruction That Supports Neural Development.* Current understanding of the social nature of the brain (Cozolino, 2006) calls for educators to reexamine instructional frameworks to ensure that they promote students' neural development. Teens learn best in environments characterized by safe, caring relationships; meaningful collaboration; and frequent opportunities to engage in activities that integrate concepts and ideas across disciplines. Although many recommended practices are compatible with these goals, trauma-sensitive schools rely on differentiated instruction and dialogic teaching because of the clear benefits they offer students with early trauma histories. Differentiated instruction provides teens with frequent opportunities to give and receive feedback, thereby allowing teachers to continually adapt instruction to meet students' changing needs (Tomlinson, 2001). Dialogic teaching offers teachers a framework for addressing the language deficits that are common among this population of students (Nystrand, 2006). In addition, its commitment to conversational engagement with the teacher helps teens make connections between language and behavior, correct cognitive distortions, and build personal agency into their explanatory narratives.

*Classroom Management.* Trauma-sensitive schools use components of positive peer culture (PPC) and positive behavior support (PBS) to help students achieve self-regulatory behaviors, make positive connections with others, and develop self-esteem. Knowing that adolescence is a period of development in which family relationships are overshadowed by the emergence of "an age segregated peer group" (Bronfenbrenner, 2005, p. 231), staff members in trauma-sensitive schools rely on classroom management techniques modeled after positive peer culture (PPC). This evidence-based peer helping model is designed to improve social competence and cultivate teen strengths (Vorrath & Brendtro, 1985). Strategies borrowed from PPC use the power of the peer group to cultivate care and concern for others. Support from empathic adults helps students develop personal responsibility and empowers them to discover their internal strength and greatness. Positive caring norms are established as part of the school culture. These counter any tendency toward antisocial activities such as bullying, while reinforcing prosocial attitudes, beliefs, and behaviors. The PPC model adopted by trauma-sensitive schools intentionally fosters relationships based on peer concern rather than peer coercion. Emphasis is placed on increasing students' awareness of the effects of their actions on self and others. Group problem solving and collaboration help teens improve their executive functioning skills and encourages them to treat others with empathy and respect.

The PBS model is an extension of applied behavior analysis that anticipates when and where problem behaviors may occur throughout the school day (Sugai et al., 2000). It is a tiered approach that focuses on preventing behaviors that are inconsistent with school success. School-based teams identify a limited number of developmentally appropriate behaviors that staff and students work on together throughout the day. Expectations are clearly defined and frequently discussed, using a common language that reinforces the model's focus on anticipating and preventing problems. Students can access universal supports–that is, supports needed to meet agreed-upon expectations–across all school settings on an as-needed basis. Trauma-sensitive schools emphasize supports that help teens manage stress, avoid trauma triggers, and build positive relationships with teachers and peers.

*Policies and Procedures.* Trauma-sensitive schools are characterized by policies and procedures designed to ensure the safety and success of students who are struggling to manage the effects of trauma. Though physical safety is paramount, the approach also includes strict adherence to confidentiality and protection against bullying and other threats to emotional well-being. Clear rules apply to communication with noncustodial parents, especially when there is a restraining order or a history of domestic violence.

Policies regarding discipline, safety planning, communication, and collaboration with community health organizations benefit not only students with known histories of trauma but also those whose trauma will never be clearly defined, as well as those who may be affected by the behavior of their traumatized classmates (Asam, 2015).

*Discipline.* Discipline policies in trauma-sensitive schools are proactive, intended to anticipate and prevent as many problems as possible. Staff members are trained to implement agreed-upon universal supports in a consistent and timely manner. Teachers articulate and review behavioral expectations with students. The school handles infractions in a collaborative manner that increases teens' self-awareness and their ability to monitor their behaviors. Conflicts are resolved in a manner that repairs any harm that may have occurred.

*Collaboration with Community Agencies.* To address the mental health needs of students and families with trauma histories or current adversities, trauma-sensitive school policies include protocols that create formal collaborative relationships with community mental health agencies. These partnerships increase opportunities for social–emotional interventions, provide school staff with convenient referral services, and offer training for teachers and school staff.

The benefits of a trauma-sensitive approach go beyond the intended goal of helping traumatized youth achieve academic and social competency. The model also helps students who are unaffected by trauma by reducing disruptive behaviors that pose a threat to school safety and often derail classroom instruction and time on task. As teachers learn new strategies to address the needs of traumatized teens, they become better equipped to meet the emotional needs of all of their students. They are able to garner professional support from their peers and are not afraid to ask for help when they need it.

## IMPLICATIONS FOR EDUCATIONAL REFORM

The first step in implementing a trauma-informed approach in schools is to acknowledge the scope of the problem. Although schools have come a long way in normalizing other types of learning and behavior problems, those that appear to be in some way related to family functioning are approached more gingerly, if at all.

The "conspiracy of silence" that surrounds children and adolescent trauma manifests in the way traditional schools respond to trauma victims. Screenings for adverse childhood experiences or developmental histories that include questions about early traumatic experiences are seldom, if ever, used in schools. Teachers are hesitant to probe too deeply into the lives of students outside of school, either because they fear reprisal from parents or because they see it as outside the scope of their work. In the absence of these data, it is estimated that each year in the United States more than a million children and adolescents are diagnosed with a mental illness or disability that could be better explained by trauma (Leahy, 2015). Some of these youth are placed in alternative schools or juvenile justice facilities (Levine & Kline, 2006), while others receive special education services or medications that do not meet their needs because they do not treat the underlying trauma.

Rather than turning a blind eye to the adversity in students' lives, staff members in trauma-sensitive schools are equipped to bear witness to its existence. In this non-stigmatizing environment, youth experience a sense of belonging and acceptance that is missing in other environments where they feel marginalized and alone. No longer needing to hide the stress in their lives, they are able to develop the skills they need to move beyond trauma and create a future for themselves. Validating students' life experiences in nonjudgmental ways is the cornerstone of a trauma-sensitive approach.

## WHAT ADMINISTRATORS CAN DO

1. Provide staff with professional development training on how to de-escalate hostile, aggressive behaviors.
2. Provide staff with professional development training on differentiated instruction and dialogic teaching.
3. Provide the leadership needed to help staff arrive at a limited number of developmentally appropriate expectations for students.
4. Be clear, consistent, and fair with regard to rules and expectations (these rules and expectations should be informed by students). Any deviation from classroom and schoolwide rules and expectations by an adult will undermine the sense of community trauma-sensitive schools hope to achieve.
5. Review school policies to ensure that they reflect a trauma-informed approach.
6. Ensure that every student has an advisor.
7. Establish learning support teams (LSTs) to locate school and local resources, including agencies that provide family and youth health

and mental health services; identify school needs and existing resources; and coordinate service delivery across programs and settings. (For more information, visit the UCLA Center for Mental Health in the Schools: www.smhp.psych.ucla.ed)

---

### WHAT TEACHERS CAN DO

1. Focus on getting to know the strengths and interests of just one "tough" student.

2. Willingly collaborate with students to develop the social and regulatory behaviors they need to achieve academic and social mastery.

3. Use clear, precise language to talk to students about how they can work with you to anticipate and prevent problems.

4. Remain objective when de-escalating students' aggressive behavior.

5. Use differentiated instruction and dialogic teaching to design lessons that engage children in meaningful activities that foster neural development and higher-order thinking.

## CONCLUSION

Experiences of early childhood and/or ongoing trauma threaten the academic and social success of students throughout adolescence. The fact that trauma changes brain architecture in ways that are detrimental to learning is well established. The trauma-sensitive schools movement represents a national effort to adapt trauma-informed approaches to educational reform. These include designing instruction in a manner that promotes neural development, consistent use of positive behavioral supports, collaboration with community mental professionals, and creation of a school climate that ensures safety for all youth. Staff members are able to work with the brain's adaptive capacity or neuroplasticity to help students recover their capacity for self-regulation, social connection, and learning. Those students are then able to look forward to leading healthy and productive adult lives.

# CHAPTER 2

# Addressing the Many Faces of Adolescent Trauma

> The most important question in the world is "why is the child crying?"
>
> —Alice Walker

The word *traumatic* is often used to describe extraordinary events such as the Bastille Day bombings on July 14, 2016, or the June 12, 2016, Orlando nightclub shootings. This usage is imprecise, however. Events are not traumatic in and of themselves; they become traumatic when they exceed a person's capacity to cope. In other words, trauma depends not only on the event, but also on the availability of resources that can help a person respond to the situation, manage their reaction, and regain a sense of equanimity and control.

This chapter describes the prevalence of trauma and its effects on adolescent development, the traumatizing effects of marginalization, and suggestions for what schools can do to heal trauma by creating more inclusive learning environments.

## THE PREVALENCE OF TRAUMA AND ITS EFFECTS ON ADOLESCENT NEURAL DEVELOPMENT

The prevalence of trauma and victimization among teenagers is shocking. Of the 76 million youth living in the United States, about 46 million are trauma survivors (Pickens, Siegfried, Surko, & Dierkhising, 2016). Evidence from three separate, but closely related, lines of work on adverse childhood experiences (Felitti et al., 1998), polyvictimization (Finkelhor, Ormrod, & Turner, 2007), and cumulative trauma (Briere & Spinazzola, 2005; Cloitre et al., 2009), provides strong support for a correlation between trauma histories and subsequent academic and social problems that persist well into adolescence.

The Adverse Childhood Experiences (ACE) study provides substantial evidence of the role that trauma and cumulative stress play in increasing the risk of disease, disability, and early mortality (Felitti et al., 1998). The

ACE study distinguished itself from earlier investigations of the relationship between trauma and disease or dysfunction in several important ways. First, it looked only at interpersonal adversity, excluding other traumatic events such as accidents or natural disasters. Second, it increased the range of potentially traumatic experiences to include household dysfunction and family mental health, as well as examples of abuse and neglect. Third, it looked at the cumulative effects of repeated "hidden stressors" rather than just single traumatic events.

The ACE study shows that adverse childhood experiences (see Figure 2.1) are much more common than recognized or previously acknowledged. The results offer substantial evidence that chronic stress at an early age overtaxes the body's biological systems and alters a host of stress-related responses in ways that are detrimental to development.

Since it was first conceptualized, the ACEs pyramid (see Figure 2.2) has been revised (see Figure 2.3), first to include scientific breakthroughs in the understanding of how chronic childhood adversity affects early brain development (Center for Youth Wellness, 2014), and more recently has been

## Figure 2.1. Types of Adverse Childhood Experiences

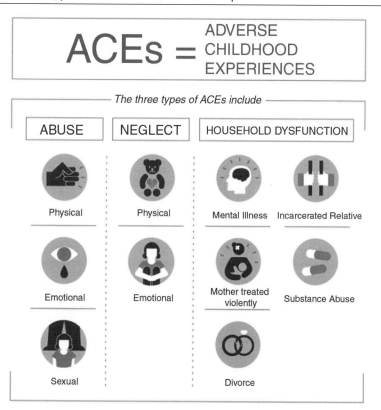

Figure 2.2. Original ACE Pyramid

Figure 2.3. Revised ACE Pyramid

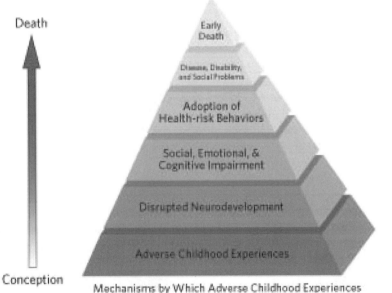

expanded (see Figure 2.4) to include adversity related to one's social location, specifically structures that embody historical trauma and contextual inequities (Stevens, 2015).

Figure 2.4. Expanded ACE Pyramid

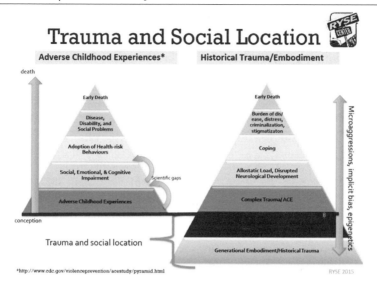

## The Multiple Effects of Polyvictimization

The term *polyvictimization* grew out of a large, nationally representative random digit dial survey of caregivers of children 2–9 and adolescents 10–17
(Turner, Finkelhor & Ormrod, 2010). Random digital dialing is a commonly
used statistical method for selecting interview subjects by randomly generating
a list of telephone numbers. Its use increases the reliability of the findings as
compared to other sampling techniques. Victimization was measured using
the juvenile victimization questionnaire (JVQ) (Hamby, Finkelhor, Turner, &
Kracke, 2011). Like the ACE study, the authors of the adolescent victimization study focused only on interpersonal events and the effects of multiple
or cumulative incidences of victimization. And the results were similar. The
JVQ study demonstrated that when estimating children's risk for the symptoms of posttraumatic stress disorder (PTSD), researchers need to consider the
total number of ways children were victimized within a calendar year rather
than focusing on any single type alone (Finkelhor, Ormrod, Turner, & Hamby,
2010).

## The Cumulative Effects of Repeated Trauma

The effects of trauma on children and youth are cumulative. Multiple ex-
posures to interpersonal trauma, such as abandonment, betrayal, physical
or sexual assaults, or exposure to domestic violence, have consistent and
predictable consequences. These affect many areas of functioning that have
serious ramifications for academic and social mastery.

A history of early trauma interferes with neurological development (van der Kolk, 2005) and the development of core self-regulation capacities (Ford & Russo, 2006). These set the stage for lifelong unfocused responses to stress. Teens' capacity to integrate sensory, emotional, and cognitive information in new situations is compromised by their brains' response to traumatic events in the past.

Efforts to arrive at a precise diagnosis of cumulative trauma in teenagers are hampered by the vast array of developmental consequences. Multiple discrete diagnoses of problems such as attention deficit/hyperactivity disorder, speech delay, and oppositional-defiant behavior obscure the pattern of trauma-related disturbances that are part of a pervasive disorder that needs to be addressed in an integrated manner (van der Kolk, 2005).

In 2005, members of the National Child Traumatic Stress Network (NCTSN) came together to develop a more precise diagnosis for children with early trauma histories. Referred to as developmental trauma disorder (DTD), the provisional diagnosis is organized around the issues of "triggered dysregulation in response to traumatic reminders, stimulus generalization, and the anticipatory organization of behavior to prevent the recurrence of the trauma impact" (van der Kolk, 2005). These manifest in school as poor self-regulation and a propensity toward apparently unprovoked aggressive behavior, a pervasive mistrust of authority figures, and a hypersensitivity to danger that limits children's motivation and ability to learn.

The converging evidence of the ACE and JVQ studies combined with research on the consequences of cumulative trauma makes the negative impact of early adversity on students' lives impossible to ignore. Given the prevalence of trauma and victimization among teenagers, educators need strategies to help youth overcome the negative effects of these experiences. Overall, this means helping teachers appreciate the brain's never-ending plasticity–its capacity to change within the context of nurturing, social relationships.

## Changes in Brain Architecture

Coping with early trauma causes adaptations to brain architecture that influence thinking, cognitive flexibility, reaction time, and the ability to anticipate consequences. These slow the development of the prefrontal cortex and executive function. Similarly, a pattern of dysfunction in the hippocampus, amygdala, medial prefrontal cortex, and other limbic structures believed to mediate anxiety and mood dysregulation make emotional regulation more difficult for teens with early trauma histories to achieve (Teicher, Anderson, Polcari, Anderson, & Navalta, 2002).

Behaviorally, a deep-seated distrust of adults, coupled with a hypersensitivity to perceptions of danger or threat, seriously compromises adolescents' ability to learn. Instead of integrating new information or experiences, their attention is directed at survival and defending themselves against recurring trauma symptoms such as heightened arousal or dissociation. Some teens avoid situations that precipitate these symptoms. Others try to project some sense of control over potential danger or threats. These youth *reenact* their traumas through aggressive or sexual acting-out behaviors. Others develop *somatic problems*, such as headaches and stomachaches, in response to fearful and helpless emotions.

## Effects on Synaptic Pruning

Synaptic pruning is normal in adolescence. It is nature's way of increasing brain efficiency by destroying underused synapses and making room for an expanded presence of white matter through the process of myelination. Microglia, a type of nonneuronal brain cells that make up one-tenth of the cells in the brain, participate in the pruning process. These cells, which are part of the immune system, engulf and digest entire cells and cellular debris. Early trauma appears to trigger a reaction in microglial cells that stimulates the secretion of neurochemicals that cause chronic inflammation in the brain (Gentile et al., 2015). This inflammation may increase the likelihood that adolescents with early trauma histories will develop mood disorders, have poor executive functioning skills, or be predisposed to posttraumatic stress disorder (Callianeo et al., 2015).

## Effects on Systemic Integration

Achievement of academic and social mastery requires students to be able to use various parts of the brain in a reciprocal, integrated manner. This poses a serious challenge to adolescents with histories of early or ongoing adversity. They need help learning to coordinate the functioning of four important neural structures: the left and right hemispheres, the subcortical brain, and the neocortex.

Research first published at the turn of the 21st century documents how early trauma interferes with the integration of the left and right hemispheres (Crittenden, 1998; Kagan, 2002; Teicher et al., 2002). More recently, MRI imaging studies report differences between maltreated students and their typical peers in the size and volume of the corpus callosum, the band of muscle that connects the hemispheres and transmits messages between them (McCrory, De Brito, & Viding, 2011).

The right hemisphere is very active in early childhood, absorbing bodily sensations, reactions to early interactions with caregivers, and strong emotions that can feel overwhelming at times. Caregivers who teach children words to describe or name their feelings help develop the left hemisphere's capacity to label right hemisphere data. Once the left hemisphere comes online, children are able to sort, select, and sequence the experiences of their inner lives into a coherent narrative.

Children whose caregivers are unaware of language's regulating function often fail to link words and experiences. As a result, the right and left hemispheres are unable to work together to manage and explain the emotional flow of the right hemisphere (McCrory, De Brito, & Viding, 2011; van der Kolk, 2003). This integration failure is the cause of much of the emotional dysregulation and disruptive behavior observed in adolescents with early or ongoing trauma histories. When stressed, these teens experience disintegration of their analytic, language-mediated left hemisphere. Their emotional, nonverbal right hemisphere takes over, causing them to react with uncontrollable terror and dismay.

The effects of trauma on the coordination of information passing between the subcortical brain and the neocortex is similar to what is observed between the left and right hemispheres. Chronic exposure to fearful stimuli affects the development of the hippocampus, left cerebral cortex, and the cerebellar vermis in ways that are detrimental to children's ability to integrate sensory input. As a result, the ability of the cortex to help adolescents modulate the subcortical response to fear and danger is compromised (van der Kolk, 2003).

Within community and school environments, these teens are hypervigilant, always on the lookout for possible threats or rejection. They often display symptoms of compulsive repetition or the need to engage authority figures in reenactments of past traumatic exchanges with caregivers. Sustaining positive interactions with these adolescents requires significant objectivity and an ability to resist personalizing their hostility and disrespect. Reframing these behaviors as symptoms of underlying terror helps, as does knowing how to de-escalate behavior by engaging youth in collaborative dialogue about what is going on for them.

Students with early or ongoing trauma histories need many opportunities to practice skills that strengthen the neural pathways linking their behavior and their prefrontal cortex. Frequent participation in activities that require higher-order thinking help make the necessary connections. If necessary, teachers can provide the scaffolds youth need to collaborate with others and solve difficult problems. Without these opportunities to strengthen the brain's executive functioning, these adolescents will be unable to override the reactivity of the subcortical brain in situations that require it.

## TRAUMA AND MARGINALIZATION

The daily experience of many adolescents is characterized not only by frequent exposure to traumatic events (Breslau, Wilcox, Storr, Lucia, & Anthony, 2004; Singer, Anglin, Song, & Lunghofe, 1995), but also poverty, diminished social resources, racial discrimination, chaotic living conditions, and social marginalization (Jones, Hadder, Carvajal, Chapman, & Alexander, 2006; Schneier, 2006).

Social marginalization is the process whereby something or someone is pushed to the edge of a group and accorded lesser importance. It occurs as a result of cultural bias: a composite of assumptions, values, and patterns of be-havior that individuals or groups define as real, true, or absolute. In schools, cultural bias shapes beliefs about knowledge and the purpose of instruction and defines preferred methods and legitimate forms of assessment. Powerful as it is, cultural bias often goes unnoticed or not reflected upon, especially in homogeneous neighborhoods and institutions. Often referred to as implicit bias, these attitudes and beliefs are so ingrained that they are thought of as truth by those who hold them (Hammond, 2015). Mutually reinforcing poli-cies and practices develop across social, economic, educational, and political domains with little awareness of how these contribute to unequal opportu-nities among those whose values or life experiences are different from those of the majority.

As of the school year 2011–2012, 18.5% of school districts had a majority of minority students enrolled. In 2014, the percentage of non-White minority students enrolled in public schools reached 50.3%, making them the majori-ty nationwide (Maxwell, 2014). Though school enrollment demographics are changing dramatically, teacher demographics have remained at about 82% White, 8% Hispanic, 7% Black, 3% Other (NCES, 2016). Addressing these contrasting demographics between students and teachers requires a cultural-ly relevant pedagogy that addresses implicit bias and considers the cultures of students in deciding how those students should be taught (Ladson-Billings, 1995). Schools can no longer assume that traditional classroom instruction will address the needs of the students enrolled in them. To do so would be to mis-represent education as assimilation into a no-longer-majority White culture.

## Marginalization of Students of Color

Unexplored implicit bias in schools negatively affects students of color when their abilities and contributions to classroom discussions are repeatedly dismissed or ignored by staff (Boykin & Noguera, 2011). Subtle, seeming-ly innocuous verbal or behavioral messages that denigrate or hurt students of color are commonplace in many schools (Kohli & Solórzano, 2012). Al-though these "micro-aggressions" are not consciously racist, they can be compared to "death by a million tiny cuts" (Griffin, 2015). They demean the experience of students of color, and make them question their capacity to achieve academic or social mastery. Examples of commonly experienced micro-aggressions include receiving more severe punishments than White students who engage in the same behavior (Rudd, 2015), the expectation that Black students will be better athletes than academics (Griffin, 2015), having cultural artifacts that are important to students' collective identities dismissed or barred from the classroom (Emdin, 2016), and accusations of "playing the race card" when citing experiences of discrimination toward themselves or a family member (Hammond, 2015).

Experiences of micro-aggressions exacerbate the mental health prob-lems of adolescents with early trauma histories. Common symptoms include depression, anxiety, negative affect, and lack of behavioral control (Nadal, Griffin, Wong, & Rasmus, 2014). Knowing this, staff in trauma-sensitive schools are trained to be aware of their own biases and to work with colleagues to notice and address micro-aggressions when they occur. They are comfortable addressing situations that appear to make one or more students uncomfortable, and are committed to improving teens' cultural awareness.

## Marginalization of LGBTQ Students

Despite the progress that continues to be made to ensure equal rights for sexual minorities, LGBTQ youth are routinely harassed because of their sexual orientation. The 2013 National School Climate Survey, the only national survey of students who identify as LGBTQ in America's secondary schools, reports widespread marginalization of this population (Glsen, 2015). In a sample of 7,898 middle and high school students, 74.1% of LGBTQ students experienced verbal harassment at school in the past year because of their sexual orientation, 55.5% felt unsafe at school because of their sexual orientation, and 30.3% skipped a day of school in the past month because of safety concerns due to sexual orientation (GLSEN, 2015). LGBTQ youth are nearly twice as likely to be called names, verbally harassed, or physically assaulted at school compared to their non-LGBTQ peers (Human Rights Campaign, 2013). These acts of bullying are not only student-to-student incidents: In a national survey, nearly a third of transgender respondents reported being verbally harassed by teachers or staff in a K–12 school, 5% reported being physically assaulted by these adults, and 3% reported being sexually assaulted.

Staff in trauma-sensitive schools know that creating an inclusive, safe school environment for LGBTQ youth involves creating gay/straight alliances that disseminate information about sexual orientation and encourage communication among all students. Contributions of LGBTQ people are integrated into content areas, and important historical landmarks such as the Stonewall riots (1969) and the Marriage Equality Act (2015) are acknowledged. Gender-neutral language is used in written materials sent to families, and same-sex parents are welcome members of the school community.

## Marginalization of Immigrant, Undocumented, and Refugee Students

The experiences of immigrant and refugee youth include a variety of challenges that leave them socially disadvantaged and only marginally engaged with their peers. Many have endured difficult migration experiences or face the uncertainty of undocumented status (Arbona et al., 2010). Almost all face resettlement issues that require them to assume adult roles and responsibilities at home. These include caring for younger siblings as parents struggle with unemployment, underemployment, and/or double-shift work—stressors that readily translate into financial distress, parental absences, and the need for the newcomer youth to work (Sefa Dei, 2016). In addition, they struggle with linguistic barriers, acculturation difficulties, adaptation challenges, and experiences of social isolation (Segal, 2011). At school, nonrecognition of prior schooling, interruptions or changes in schooling, differential educational levels, lack of familiarity with the U.S. school system and practices, mismatches between home and school cultural values, and unwelcoming school environments often present additional challenges for these students.

Trauma-sensitive schools recognize the unique stresses faced by this population of students, which sometimes includes a history of potentially traumatic experiences. Emphasis is placed on creating compassionate learning environments that facilitate relationships with peers, while at the same time providing intensive support for learning English, developing academic skills and content knowledge, and adjusting to life in the United States. Wherever possible, instructional tasks include group work, interactive lessons, and activities that encourage acceptance and diversity among the students.

## HEALING TRAUMA THROUGH INCLUSION: WHAT SCHOOLS CAN DO

Trauma-sensitive schools are committed to creating a spirit of inclusion that celebrates individual differences. Participation in a diverse learning community provides teens with frequent opportunities for peer collaboration and support. These activities foster empathy and perspective taking while gently challenging preconceived notions that peers may have of one another. Close collaboration enables students to work within their zone of proximal development with others' support. Within this context, they are able to reap the benefits of important changes in their neural development.

### Harness Neuroplasticity

The neuroplasticity that characterizes adolescent neurobiology offers teens the opportunity to move beyond the reactivity of the reptilian brain toward the development of one dominated by a highly efficient and well-integrated prefrontal cortex. Research suggests that progress toward dominance by the prefrontal cortex comes about by the coordination of changes in the structure and connectivity of the brain that further differentiate areas of the brain while at the same time increasing the speed at which information from different areas of the brain can be integrated (Jensen & Nutt, 2015; Siegel, 2013a; Steinberg, 2014).

To take full advantage of adolescents' neural plasticity, the cognitive demands placed on teens must exceed their brains' capacity to meet them

(Steinberg, 2014). Learning activities that are too easy or monotonous do not take advantage of neuroplasticity. Rather, academic tasks must be within teens' zone of proximal development: achievable, but only within a social context, with support from others (Vygotsky, 1986). Schools can harness the benefits of neuroplasticity for adolescents by collaborating with them to support three important areas of neural development: differentiation, connectivity, and facilitating changes in the frontal/limbic balance.

*Differentiation.* The synaptic pruning that occurs in adolescence encourages the emergence of specialized areas of the brain that contribute to improved neural efficiency. Because this process occurs in a use-dependent manner, the more experiences to which adolescents are exposed, the greater capacity they have for developing neural networks that involve a host of talents and lifelong interests that increase their potential to be contributing members of society. The quality of teen experiences also matters. Teens involved in the arts, sports, or academics are hardwiring the neural connections in their brain along these areas of specialization (Giedd, 2015).

Teens with early or current trauma histories struggle to achieve neural differentiation, which in turn, slows the development of executive functions. In early childhood, attachment failures caused by inadequate caregiving, combined with other forms of childhood adversity, deny these teens the confidence needed to explore their interests or encounter new experiences as pleasurable, thereby narrowing their range of activities. The lack of safety in their immediate environment directs their attention toward survival, resulting in adaptions to their stress response that limit their ability to learn. As a result, in adolescence they are ill-equipped to know what interests them or how to pursue a variety of experiences that could increase their potential for developing a highly differentiated neural system.

Much like early childhood, the teenage years are a period where access to enrichment activities and brain-stimulating experiences hold the promise of enhanced cognitive development (Giedd, 2015; Jensen & Nutt, 2015; Siegel, 2013a; Steinberg, 2014). Trauma-sensitive secondary schools ensure that students have equitable exposure to a wide range of extracurricular and enrichment activities. These enable teens with early or current trauma histories to try new things and nurture talents that support their neural development and enhance the quality of their lives.

*Connectivity.* What lies at the core of adolescent cognitive development is the attainment of a more fully conscious, self-directed, and self-regulating mind. This is achieved principally through the maturation of an advanced set of executive functions, rather than through specific improvement of any one in particular (Steinberg, 2007). Much of the underlying action is focused on specific developments in the prefrontal cortex and its rapidly expanding linkages to other areas of the brain. These represent a shift from childhood's less well-integrated neural processing toward the development of neural networks that are capable of more sophisticated and intricate functions. These networks are formed by the complementary processes of pruning and myelination that occur in adolescents, and greatly enhance teens' capacity for higher-order thinking and information-processing speed.

The hypothalamus-pituitary-adrenal (HPA) axis controls important bodily functions including the body's stress system and one's capacity for self-regulatory behaviors. The hypothalamus is a part of the brain which links the nervous system to the endocrine system via the pituitary and adrenal glands. Adolescence is marked by increased stress reactivity in the HPA axis. Stress-sensitive cortical brain areas such as the prefrontal cortex that continue to mature during adolescence may be particularly vulnerable to these shifts in stress reactivity (Jensen & Nutt, 2015; Siegel, 2013a; Steinberg, 2014; van der Kolk, 2003). Trauma-sensitive schools integrate stress management activities into daily activities and routines in an effort to provide adolescents with a learning environment that optimizes their neural development. Students are encouraged to develop their own stress management plans. For some, this means finding healthy ways to release tension. For others, it means using visualization to "travel" to a beautiful, relaxing place. Many find practicing yoga or martial arts helpful stress management techniques. Teens are encouraged to experiment with different methods until they find one that works for them.

*Frontal/Limbic Balance.* During adolescence, the regulatory systems of the reptilian brain are gradually brought under the control of central executive functions, as the maturing prefrontal cortex inhibits impulsivity and enables teens to achieve greater levels of self-regulation than were previously available to them (Diamond, 2013; Jensen & Nutt, 2015; Siegel, 2013a; Steinberg, 2014). This conscious control of regulatory capacities is, however, not a skill set that comes online quickly. It is a lengthy process that requires the sustained support of adults who are available to collaborate with teens in a manner that strengthens the neural pathways responsible for impulse control and rational decisionmaking.

## Provide Nonparental Adult Support

Adult mentoring and support is particularly important for teens whose daily lives are burdened with adversity and emotionally laden dilemmas from a relatively early age. Though adolescence is typically a period when teens push back from their parents, this shift toward autonomy should not be construed as an indication that adults have no role to play in teens' lives (Siegel, 2013a). Rather, it suggests the very real need for nonparental adults to engage teens in positive and constructive ways. Youth interact with nonparental adults in a more mature manner. They tend to listen more closely to adults other than their parents, sometimes even accepting their advice and redirection.

In terms of developing self-regulatory skills, the inclusion of nonparental adults in teens' lives offers unique opportunities to engage in relationships that help teens acquire the dispositions and skills they need to take charge of their lives. The protective nature of these partnerships shields teens from the suboptimal trajectories that might befall them in the absence of a fully developed set of executive functions.

Knowing the importance of adult relationships in helping teens acquire cortical/limbic balance and coordination, staff members in trauma-sensitive secondary schools are committed to creating and sustaining a relationship-based culture. They use formal and informal supports to ensure that all students have easy access to adults who care about them and are willing to problem-solve with them. In middle schools, formal supports usually involve homeroom meetings at the beginning or end of the day, whereas in high schools, advisory periods and mentoring programs serve this purpose.

Advisory periods are regularly scheduled opportunities for a staff member and a small number of students to meet to share information and experiences that affect life at school. A key function of the advisory is to ensure that all students have an adult who knows them and is able to represent their concerns to other members of the school community.

Mentoring involves a one-on-one, supportive relationship between a student and an adult. Although not all students in trauma-sensitive schools require individualized support, it is available for those who are in crisis or transitioning from other specialized or court-directed programs. Mentoring is associated with improving a student's connection to school and adults, and improving dropout indicators and higher achievement (Shapiro, Oesterle, & Hawkins, 2015).

Informal supports include a commitment to staff visibility throughout the day: greeting students in the morning, mingling with them in the cafeteria or student lounge, saying good-bye at the end of the day. In both middle schools and high schools, students are referred to by name and acknowledged by staff when passing one another in hallways. These repeated acts of acknowledgment and respect show students they are valued members of the school community.

## IMPLICATIONS FOR EDUCATIONAL REFORM

By adolescence, trauma-sensitive intervention requires the acknowledgment of not only the individual trauma experienced by students, but also trauma endured as a result of their collective identity and marginalization. The degree to which teens are victimized demands assertive efforts by educational leaders to protect them from harassment, bullying, and polyvictimization. Cultural competence and social justice need to inform school policies and be a driving force in the recruitment of new teachers.

Reform efforts must emphasize the importance of collaborative relationships between traumatized youth and the adults who are responsible for them. These partnerships can help adolescents develop the necessary emotional regulation and self-confidence needed to overcome past and current adversities. With the correct type of support, teens can develop sufficient executive functioning and cognitive control to make informed choices about their behavior. Stress management and self-soothing activities can help them build their tolerance for discomfort and maintain a more functional level of arousal.

---

### WHAT ADMINISTRATORS CAN DO

1. Provide the leadership necessary to ensure a safe and affirming educational environment for all students. Elicit the support of all staff in maintaining a bully-free milieu for all students.
2. Foster a nonjudgmental school climate that is sympathetic to adolescent adversity and capable of responding to it in a compassionate and affirming manner.
3. Foster a school climate that celebrates individual differences.
4. Sponsor schoolwide opportunities to increase cultural awareness among all members of the school community.
5. Provide ongoing professional development on how to design and implement culturally competent instruction.
6. Provide teachers with professional development focused on recognizing and responding to symptoms of adolescent trauma.
7. Provide ongoing professional development on the traumatizing effects of micro-aggressions on marginalized students.
8. Work with district curriculum specialists to integrate the contributions of marginalized groups into all content areas.
9. Eliminate discipline practices that may trigger symptoms in children with early trauma histories: public reprimands, time-out, zero-tolerance policies.
10. Get to know the students in your school. Greet them at the beginning and end of each day, and address them by name when passing them in hallways. Repeated positive acknowledgment can help lessen their distrust and fear of authority figures.
11. Collaborate with local community organizations to create wrap-around services for families and children who need them.
12. Schedule time for teachers to participate in professional learning communities or other interactive forums that encourage them to integrate trauma-sensitive approaches into their classroom practice.

| WHAT TEACHERS CAN DO |
| --- |

1. Become knowledgeable about the ways trauma affects adolescents' ability to achieve academic and social mastery.
2. Collaborate with children to help them manage their emotional reactions and maintain optimal levels of arousal.
3. Get to know your students. Find out what matters to them and integrate topics of interest into content instruction.
4. Be aware of students' preferences in art, music, and personal style. Find ways of representing these within the classroom.
5. Monitor the length and complexity of homework assignments to reduce unnecessary stress for teens who may be caring for siblings or working after school to help support their families.
6. Provide students with time to regain their composure before asking them to use language to explain misbehavior.
7. Design instruction that works with the brain's plasticity to strengthen the neural pathways associated with higher-order thinking.
8. Use classroom activities to foster positive relationships and social support among peers.
9. Create a safe space for marginalized students. Don't ask teens to self-identify and be mindful of your language; say *undocumented* rather than *illegal* and avoid terms like *alien* or *legal immigration*.
10. Do all you can to identify *yourself* as an ally/supporter of marginalized students. Use posters, bookmarks, and stickers to make your support visible Examples are available online at www.e4fc.org/onlinestore.html

## CONCLUSION

The high prevalence of early trauma, trauma histories, and polyvictimization among adolescents, as well as the marginalization of many youth as a result of their minority or cultural status, is well documented. Heightened anxiety is a frequent reaction to victimization, which only exacerbates the elevated stress reactivity common in all teenagers. Experiences of bias or discrimination can further compromise students' efforts to achieve academic and social mastery. When teachers create inclusive learning environments that are capable of harnessing the power of the brain's neuroplasticity, they help teens learn to regulate their stress response and participate successfully in school.

# CHAPTER 3

# Remodeling the Adolescent Brain for Adulthood

> The hope for our future lies in the courage and creativity of adolescents.
>
> —Daniel Siegel

Adolescence is a period of significant changes in the brain. Important shifts occur in the limbic area, affecting teen attachment patterns, as well as their emotions, judgment, and motivation. The cortex and prefrontal cortex areas develop in a use-dependent manner, meaning that the more often life experiences stimulate these areas, the more efficient and reliable the corresponding neural circuits become (Siegel, 2013a). The activities in which youth frequently participate during adolescence shape brain function throughout the life span. How teens spend their time guides the hardwiring of adaptive connections in key areas of the brain, including the brain stem, the limbic system, the cortex, and prefrontal cortex (Giedd, 2004; Siegel, 2013a).

In the case of teenagers with early trauma histories, the heightened environmental sensitivity experienced during this period can exacerbate preexisting issues with stress reactivity, social isolation, and suicidal ideation. These teens require the support of a caring school community, mastery of increasingly complex tasks, and opportunities to form reciprocal relationships with others to help them move beyond past adversities toward a productive and meaningful future.

## NEURAL DEVELOPMENT IN ADOLESCENCE

Adolescence is similar to early childhood in terms of the significance of the brain's growth and development (Fuhrmann, Knoll, & Blakemore, 2015)). As children start their "second dozen years of life," their brains begin a period of gradual change that continues through the mid-20s. Nearly every aspect of the brain is involved in a rapid growth of nerve cells, accompanied by an increase in the number of synapses (connections between nerve cells). This increased connectivity results in a growth spurt of memory and intellectual capacity. This heightened aptitude for learning and exploration is nature's way of helping teenagers make the transition to adulthood (Anderson, 2016).

In addition to changes in cell volume and connectivity, the hormonal environment of the brain also changes during adolescence. For example, the baseline level of dopamine, the neurotransmitter most responsible for feelings of pleasure, is lower in adolescents. But its release in response to experience is higher, which perhaps explains why teens need more exciting and stimulating activities to achieve the same level of pleasure that adults routinely experience (Spear, 2013).

## Changes in the Brain Stem and Limbic Areas of the Brain

The brain stem and limbic system represent the more reactive areas of the brain. The brain stem is triggered in the face of perceived threat, activating the familiar "fight, flight, or freeze" response. The body downshifts into survival mode, unable to return to normal functioning until the threat is removed. The limbic system works with the body and brain stem to enable important neural functions. Working in tandem they generate emotions; enable bonding or attachment; and affect memory, motivation, and judgment (Siegel, 2013a).

*Emotions.* During adolescence, the limbic system exerts more influence on the cortical areas of the brain than during childhood or adulthood. The potential of this system to trigger emotions explains why adolescents sometimes appear to have "over-the-top" reactions to the neutral behaviors of others.

*Attachment.* Unlike early childhood, when the attachment process centers on the caregiver/child relationship, in adolescence same-aged peers become the important attachment figures. Just as young children delight in the presence of caring parents, teens are hardwired to experience intense pleasure just being in the company of their peers (Steinberg, 2014).

Safety and synchronicity are paramount in children's first attachment to caregivers. Within this protective relationship, children use the caregiver's support and encouragement to regulate their behavior and get their needs met (Greenspan, 1997; Schore, 1994; Siegel, 1999). The safer children feel, the more interested they become in exploring their environment. Secure in the protection afforded by the attachment relationship, they expand their range of interests and their tolerance of new situations (Fosha, 2003).

A parallel process occurs in adolescent attachment, as teens seek out peers with similar interests and ideas to form a protective tribe or posse with whom they can collaborate and explore the meaning of interpersonal relationships. The attraction of the peer group is driven in part by a need for social engagement and in part to validate teens' own beliefs and hopes for the future. The sense of being "seen" and understood by peers is not unlike the sense of safety experienced by the infant whose caregiver anticipates and meets his or her needs. It is an experience of belonging that encourages youth in middle school and high school to explore new opportunities, confident in their ability to handle the challenge of increased responsibilities and demands on their time.

*Motivation.* Dopamine is the neurotransmitter that provides the motivation to seek out rewarding, "feel-good" experiences. Dopamine levels in adolescence are lower than during childhood or adulthood. This accounts for the apparent lack of motivation among teenagers, as well as their frequent bouts of boredom. However, although it takes more to trigger a dopamine release in teens, the positive feelings associated with its discharge into the nervous system are greater than those experienced during any other period of life. The pleasure experienced by this dopamine rush is so intense that teens' attention is continually directed toward repeating it through the pursuit of novelty and excitement regardless of any risk involved (Steinberg, 2014).

*Appraisal/Judgment.* The drive toward pleasurable experiences despite the risks involved is further strengthened by the fact that teenagers' thought processes are hyperrational (Siegel, 2013b). The appraisal centers of the adolescent brain highlight and amplify the positive aspects of an experience, while minimizing the potentially negative ones. Decisions are made on the chance that everything will be fine. In the teen's mind, chances of a negative outcome are 5% while there is a 95% chance of a positive outcome (Siegel, 2013b). The danger is that although this type of hyperrational thinking may accurately assess probabilities, it also de-emphasizes the severity of the negative outcome, simply because there's only a slight chance it will happen. The desire for the pleasure of the experience obscures any potential danger that exists.

## Changes in the Cerebral Cortex

The cerebral cortex is the part of the cerebrum often referred to as the "mind." It is made up of four lobes, all of which are associated with higher brain functions: voluntary movement, coordination of sensory information, learning, memory, and personality (see Figure 3.1). The frontal lobe, and particularly the area referred to as the prefrontal cortex, undergoes extraordinary changes during adolescence, as teens increase their capacity for higher-order thinking and executive functioning (Siegel, 2013b; Weinberger, Elvevag, & Giedd, 2005).

These changes occur as the result of two complementary processes—pruning and myelination—that together improve the brain's connectivity.

Figure 3.1. Frontal Lobe

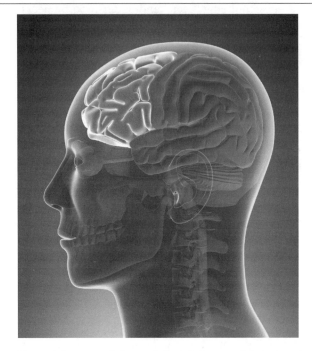

*Pruning.* Part of the remodeling of the adolescent brain involves pruning away synaptic connections and some neurons that are not used or needed. Though necessary for the development of a more efficient, integrated system, pruning marks a transition from a seemingly endless realm of possibilities in childhood to a more specialized or differentiated neural framework in adolescence and adulthood (Jensen & Nutt, 2015; Siegel, 2013a).

Although the purpose of synaptic pruning is to prepare the brain for successful adaptation and more sophisticated functioning in adulthood, it is not without its risks. Nonneuronal cells known as microglia participate in the pruning process. Their purpose is to engulf and digest cells (McCarthy, 2013). Experiences of childhood trauma appear to fire up microglia cells, causing them to produce neurochemicals that lead to neuro-inflammation, which increases the likelihood of mood disorders and poor executive functioning throughout the life span. Reducing the number of synaptic connections may also account for an increased risk of mental illness among adolescents, and is known to increase teens' stress reactivity and sensitivity to drugs (Steinberg, 2014). Also, the reduction in gray matter that occurs in pruning reduces the range of possibilities available for teens to pursue as neural connections become more differentiated in a use-dependent manner.

*Myelination.* Myelination occurs concurrently with synaptic pruning. Myelination (see Figure 3.2) is the process of forming a sheaf of myelin–a soft, white, somewhat fatty substance—around the long shaft or elongated fibers of the neuron called the axon. Myelin is intimately involved in the fine-tuning of neuron transmission, strengthening the connections between them and enabling faster, more coordinated communication among them. As myelination proceeds, neural firing becomes as much as 3,000 times faster than in childhood (Siegel, 2013a).

*Connectivity.* These changes in adolescent neural functioning link differentiated regions of the brain so they can work in a more integrated, efficient manner (see Figure 3.3). This improved communication and coordination among different areas of the brain strengthens adolescents' ability to regulate their emotions and think rationally. As connectivity improves, so does executive functioning, enabling teens to engage more readily in goal setting, problem solving, and responsible decisionmaking.

## CHANGES IN COGNITIVE FUNCTIONING RELATED TO NEURAL CHANGES

The neural reorganization that occurs during adolescence profoundly affects teens' cognitive functioning, particularly in the areas of executive function, social cognition, and capacity for abstract thought. These changes, coupled with increases in processing speed, are the foundation for adult cognition.

Figure 3.2. Myelination

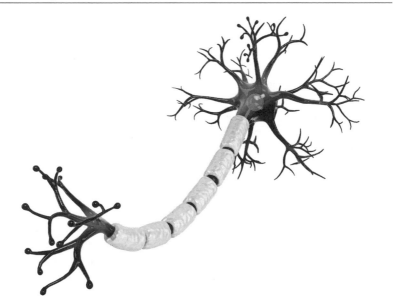

Figure 3.3. Neural Connectivity

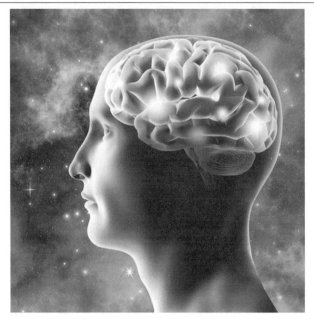

## Executive Functioning

Increased neural connectivity and maturation of the prefrontal cortex in adolescence enables a marked improvement in teens' ability to control and coordinate their thoughts and behavior (Luria, 1966). As adolescents advance through secondary school, their cognitive processing becomes increasingly reliant on the executive functions of cognitive flexibility, inhibition, and working memory. They demonstrate an increased capacity for planning and goal setting, as well as time management and organizational skills.

*Cognitive Flexibility.* The heightened dopamine reaction and accelerated neuroplasticity that occurs in adolescence drives teens' interest in novel experiences and ideas, as well as their passion for learning more about topics that interest them. Cognitive flexibility, or the ability to shift perspective in response to new data, allows them to expand their worldview, create new solutions to problems, and, overall, become more capable of collaborative partnerships with others.

Physical abuse and physical neglect are associated with diminished cognitive flexibility in adolescents (Spann et al., 2012). Rigid thinking, perseveration, and an inability to assess an experience from multiple perspectives develop as a function of early insecure attachments that prevented children's exploration of their environment. Explicit instruction in flexible thinking helps teens become more open to different perspectives, and less committed to the idea that there is only one "right" answer to every question.

Teachers in trauma-sensitive schools foster teens' cognitive flexibility by integrating divergent thinking strategies into content instruction. Some use the Role, Audience, Form, Topic (RAFT) strategy, which encourages students to explore literature and historical events from the perspective of different characters or historical figures. Other teachers encourage students to compare and contrast different versions of one of Shakespeare's plays or Vivaldi's Quartet. Students are encouraged to transfer their learning from one content area to create a novel application in another. With enough practice, students become more capable of juggling multiple perspectives and generating alternative solutions to everyday problems.

*Cognitive Control.* As the prefrontal cortex develops, adolescents increase their capacity for planning and goal-directed behavior. This occurs through the strengthening of their working memory and improvements in their ability to voluntarily control their behavior through response inhibition.

The mechanisms underlying working memory–or the ability to hold information in mind while working with part of it–develop early, but the processes underlying the fidelity of the representation kept in working memory improve through adolescence (Luna & Sweeney, 2004). Working memory helps students maintain their focus and concentration by helping them remember what they need to be paying attention to.

Inhibition involves the ability to resist engaging in a habitual response as well as the ability to ignore distracting information. It allows teens to select goal-directed behaviors while ignoring compelling, but task-inappropriate, alternatives. Inhibition provides teens with the flexibility they need to exert cognitive control over their behavior. Teens with early trauma histories often lack the cognitive flexibility needed to resist habitual responses or to ignore distractions. Trauma limits students' ability to change how they think about things, especially how they think about themselves or adults who try to help them. The hypervigilance that keeps them on the lookout for danger interferes with their ability to focus, and makes them very easily distracted.

*Time Management and Organization.* As executive functions, time management and organization rely on teens' ability to integrate their understanding of the concepts of time, sequence, and estimation to work toward personal goals. Having an accurate sense of time, along with the capacity to correctly order tasks sequentially and accurately estimate how much time each step will take to complete, helps teens perform efficiently. This success provides them with a sense of personal efficacy and confidence in their ability to get things done.

Teens with early trauma histories often have a diminished grasp of time, sequence, and estimation. Traumatic events are known to distort a sense of time, leaving victims "frozen" in the traumatic moment, without a clear sense of past, present, or future. Caregivers' lack of consistency and predictability in early childhood interferes with the development of sequential thought and estimation. As a result, these students are often observed to be "spinning their wheels," unable to sustain progress on predetermined goals or to complete tasks in a timely manner.

Staff members in trauma-sensitive schools accommodate to these deficiencies through frequent use of stylized routines, transitional rituals, and a tight adherence to the scheduling of school and classroom events. Teens are encouraged to estimate how long they think it will take to complete a task, and compare their estimates to the actual time spent. Long-term assignments are completed in agreed-upon chunks of time, and students are given teacher feedback before beginning the next section. Students are encouraged to keep daily records of their activities and collaborate with teachers to identify frequently occurring time wasters, and together find strategies they can use to avoid these in the future.

## Social Cognition

In addition to changes that affect how they think, adolescents' brains also undergo developments that affect how teens feel. Teenagers begin to empathize more with others and take into account how their actions will affect not just themselves, but the people around them.

*The Role of Mindsight.* The prefrontal cortex uses sensory input to create representations of others' minds in much the same way as it uses sensory input to create images of the physical world. Mirror neurons detect another person's intentional acts or predictable sequences and automatically "get ready" to engage in the same activity. This attunement is the basis of the social interdependence that characterizes dyadic relationships and group behavior. It is the essence of representational thought, or the ability to detect the intentional state of others.

This capacity for "mindsight" begins in early childhood (Siegel, 2011). It develops at the same time that increased verbal ability and semantic memory enable children to hold internal images of people, objects, and events in their minds even when these things are no longer present. This sense of object permanence allows children to think about others in an abstract manner, attributing motivations and feelings to their behavior. They learn to include representations of the thoughts and feelings of others in their own thinking and realize that others do likewise. These new insights into others' mental states increase children's ability to engage in shared narratives and enjoy the company of their peers.

Repeated experiences of unpredictable, inconsistent caregiving interfere with children's acquisition of mindsight or object permanence. Their inability to understand that persons or objects still exist when out of sight, or that they themselves exist in the minds of others, diminishes their capacity for representational thought and social interdependence. Lack of insight into the thoughts and feelings of others makes individuals insensitive to others' needs and incapable of sharing their perspectives.

As neural integration becomes more efficient in adolescence, teens have a second chance to acquire mindsight skill. They can be taught how to observe, consider, and voluntarily control their thinking, emotional responses, and behavior. This increased capacity for self-reflection can help them break the cycle of traumatic reenactment by getting rid of ingrained behaviors and habitual responses. With the proper guidance, they can learn to use their minds to take charge of their emotions and behavior. These mental and emotional changes are transformational at the physical level of the brain. Simply reflecting on the inner working of their minds stimulates the areas of the brain that are crucial to mental health and well-being.

*Developing Empathy.* As the brain develops, the insula, a neural circuit in the prefrontal cortex, links the activity of the mirror neurons to subcortical areas of the brain, enabling an empathic awareness toward others to emerge. This sense of physical connection with others is comprised of both affective and cognitive components. The affective component strengthens one's ability to match or join in the affective experiences of another. The cognitive component helps individuals move beyond egocentrism to the realization that others have their own experiences. Eventually, children learn to interpret the thoughts and feelings of others. The development of both the affective and cognitive aspects of empathy occur within children's early attachment relationships. In this context, they experience feelings of connection to the caregiver, as well as episodes of social rejection. In secure attachment relationships, episodes of rejecting behavior are quickly repaired by the caregiver. Reparation, however, does not occur in insecure or disorganized attachment relationships. As a result, children learn to expect to be rejected by others (Main & Solomon, 1990).

In either case, these experiences link the circuits in the brain responsible for social behavior and physical pain. These connect with the circuitry that enables children to discriminate between themselves and others. The interactions between these circuits are the basis for empathic behavior.

There is some debate as to how these neural circuits interact with one another to produce empathic thought and behaviors. "Simulation theory" (Rameson & Lieberman, 2009) favors an experiential model. Proponents argue that children use their own experiences with pain and self-soothing as a model for what others need in similar situations. When others have been a source of comfort to them, individuals are motivated to reach out to others to reduce their distress. This position is defended by the fact that the same neural structures appear to be recruited when one is personally experiencing something or observing another person in the same circumstances.

By contrast, "theory of mind" advocates take a more cognitive approach. They argue that empathic connection is the result of children's ability to think about the contents of another's mind and adjust their behavior to their perception of how the other person is feeling (Meltzoff, 2002). Mediated by the medial prefrontal cortex, empathy involves a more conscious decision about how to behave toward another. As with simulation theory, the choice of how to connect to the other person is limited by children's own experiences.

Early childhood trauma interferes with the development of empathy. As a result, adolescents with early trauma histories are less inclined than their peers to notice or seek to alleviate the distress of others. This is partly a result of their blunted affect, which both limits awareness of their own discomfort and compromises their ability to self-soothe. On the other hand, some traumatized teens can appear overly empathic, as if they are trying to alleviate their own pain by being overly solicitous of others.

The fact that trauma is associated with reduced insula volume may also contribute to the limited ability to interpret the thoughts and feelings of others observed among teens with trauma histories. They are often viewed as socially inept, behaving in a manner not unlike that seen in some students with Asperger's syndrome. Their difficulty in inferring another's feelings or intentions makes it hard for them to predict how others will think or act. This leads to errors in social cognition, as well as difficulty with inferential comprehension (van der Kolk, 2014).

## Capacity for Abstract Thinking

Adolescents' capacity for abstract thinking increases as the connectivity of the brain's neural circuits improves. Their capacity to make connections between different data sources improves and they can more easily transfer knowledge from one content area to another (Casey, Jones, & Hare, 2008). In general, abstract thinkers are able to perceive analogies and relationships that others may not see, allowing them to link new information to prior knowledge and analyze it for familiar patterns or traits. The capacity for abstract thought enables students to make generalizations across environments and transfer knowledge from one context to another.

It is unusual for students to have the same aptitude for abstraction across disciplines. Most move in and out of varying levels of abstraction and more concrete thinking. Improvements in one area do not necessarily generalize to others.

Staff members in trauma-sensitive schools recognize that within any group of adolescents there will be a variety of abilities to think abstractly. The staff, therefore, uses open-ended learning activities that accommodate these individual differences and allow students to engage the material at their own level of abstraction. Some students show a greater capacity for generalization and abstraction in some content areas, while thinking more concretely in others. Efforts to develop teens' ability for abstract thinking include teaching them how to distinguish between concrete and abstract thought processes. Staff members can use concept maps, graphic organizers, and analogies to help students build their capacity to see patterns and connections. Talking about the thought processes facilitates an understanding of those thought processes, as well as how and when to use them.

## THREATS TO SUCCESSFUL REMODELING

Although most teens are able to negotiate the many changes that occur in adolescence and enjoy its sense of freedom and opportunity, some find it a more difficult transition. These are youth who appear more vulnerable to mental illness or substance abuse. Others who struggle are those with a lack of social skills or capacity for close friendship. These teens are often isolated from peers and lack a comfortable sense of belonging. The combined stress of mental illness and social isolation can trigger suicidal ideation, and sometimes suicide attempts or death. A common risk factor for these threats to successful remodeling is a childhood history of abuse or trauma.

### Mental Illness

More than half of all mental illnesses and substance use disorders begin by age 14; three-quarters of these conditions develop by age 24 (Kessler, Berglund, Demler, Jin, Merikangas, & Waller, 2005). For youth with early trauma histories, who are at greater risk of developing mental illness than their non-traumatized peers, adolescence often marks the onset of serious mood, behavioral, and anxiety disorders.

Although questions remain about the relationship between adolescence and the onset of mental illness, likely explanations include teens' heightened stress reactivity and the possibility that synaptic pruning may reveal genetically or experientially vulnerable circuits (Siegel, 2013a). Although educational interventions to buffer the possible negative consequences of synaptic pruning are as yet unknown, schools can help adolescents manage the effects of heightened stress reactivity.

### Stress Reactivity

The environmental sensitivity that characterizes adolescence, along with heightened reactivity in the hypothalamus-pituitary-adrenal (HPA) axis (as explained in Chapter 2) that triggers the stress response and the absence of a fully developed prefrontal cortex, makes teenagers particularly vulnerable to stress (Steinberg, 2014). Hormonal changes further undermine teens' efforts at self-regulation. THP, a stress hormone that has a calming effect on children and adults in stressful situations, produces stress-triggered anxiety in adolescents (Jensen & Nutt, 2015). Cortisol levels are also slightly elevated during adolescence. These cortisol levels increase even further when teens deal with negative feelings such as loneliness or anger (Jensen & Nutt, 2015). Stress reactivity increases the adolescent risk of emotional trauma and can lead to maladaptive neurological development (Jensen & Nutt, 2015; Romeo, 2013). Without appropriate intervention, these disorders can trigger the beginning of a downward spiral of risky behaviors, school failure, self-medication, and involvement with the juvenile justice system (Murphey, Barry, & Vaughn, 2015).

Staff members in trauma-sensitive schools work with students to help them identify the different kinds of stress in their lives and develop strategies they can use to manage them. Some teens are stressed by home or community situations over which they have little control. Memories of past traumatic experiences continue to cloud the present, and they are unable to release distorted self-definitions. Learning to cope with these stresses requires relationships with adults who can help teens accept the past and reconstruct a more positive and capable self-definition. Other students are stressed by their inability to regulate their emotional responses to current situations that they find frustrating or difficult. Staff members can help these teens by equipping them with coping skills that improve their ability to seek help from others and improve their problem-solving skills.

## Social Isolation

Adolescence is the developmental period marked by a shift away from primary attachment figures and toward peers. The need to form and maintain close relationships with peers drives behavior at this age. Teens are hardwired to experience intense pleasure in the presence of their friends (Steinberg, 2014), in a manner not unlike younger children's delight in their parents' attention.

At the same time, it is a period characterized by heightened sensitivity to criticism and rapid changes in personal identity. Though the need to belong can sometimes result in poor judgment and increased risk-taking behaviors, close bonds with positive peers provide teens with the support and encouragement they need to explore who they are and what they hope to achieve. Peers help one another establish their independence, explore new interests, and test conventional boundaries, while avoiding the stress of loneliness or alienation.

The social nature of these developmental milestones makes adolescence particularly challenging for teens with early or current trauma histories. Their inherent distrust of others makes them inclined toward superficial relationships rather than close, intimate ones. Past experiences make them wary of emotional investment in peers, because they derive little pleasure from interacting with others. Difficulty integrating new information and perspective taking makes communication difficult for traumatized teens and increases the likelihood of their rejection by peers. Experiences of social rejection further destabilize their need to belong or to feel connected to and safe with others. The resulting social isolation and alienation increase their risk of being bullied or further victimized, and pose a serious threat to their well-being.

Staff members in trauma-sensitive schools work diligently to reduce teens' sense of social isolation by fostering an inclusive school climate and providing direct instruction on skills demonstrated to increase friendships. Homeroom meetings in middle school and daily advisory periods in high school provide opportunities to teach students how to communicate clearly and develop their ability to resolve conflicts. By making themselves emotionally available to students, staff members model ways of showing interest in others, how to celebrate others' successes, and how to show support during difficult times. Role-playing is used to align words with facial expressions and body language. Youth are encouraged to behave voluntarily in ways intended to benefit others. Recognizing the role that language pragmatics play in social interactions, time is spent teaching students how to initiate social interactions and how to sustain a conversation on a topic of mutual interest.

## Suicidal Ideation

Suicide is the third leading cause of death among youth ages 10–24. A history of maltreatment, domestic violence, depression, and sense of isolation are among the chief risk factors for suicide and suicidal ideation. Childhood trauma is known to cause earlier onset of psychopathology and suicidality and to lead to a cascade of other life events, each of which increases the risk for suicidality. Childhood trauma is a strong and independent risk factor for suicidal behavior in adolescents and adults (Brown & Finkelhor, 1986; Paolucci, Genuis, & Violato, 2001; Santa Mina & Gallop, 1998).

Suicide can be contagious, especially among adolescents (Abrutyn & Mueller, 2014). It is estimated that each suicide touches approximately 135 people, and about one-third of those affected experience a severe life disruption because of that suicide (Maple, Cerel, Sanford, Pearce, & Jordan, 2016). People who know the person who died of suicide are almost twice as likely to develop suicidal thoughts as the general population; adolescents are among those at greatest risk for these chain-reaction thoughts. Teens who know friends or family members who have attempted suicide are about three times more likely to attempt suicide than are teens who do not know someone who attempted suicide (Pittman, Osborn, Rantell, & King, 2016).

Although there is no empirically supported method specifically to prevent suicide, the research suggests some possible solutions. These include (1) better access to mental health services for teens with treatable risk factors such as depression and suicidal thoughts, and (2) restrictions on teen access to firearms, which are used by 66.4% of boys and 48.3% of girls who die by suicide (McIntosh, 2000). The availability of firearms in the home differentiates adolescent death by suicide (74.1%) from hospitalized adolescents who attempt suicide (33.9%) It appears that easy access to firearms increases the risk of death from suicide attempts that may otherwise have signaled a call for help but resulted in less dire consequences (Brent et al., 1988).

Staff members in trauma-sensitive schools are trained to recognize adolescent behaviors that suggest suicidal ideation and the risk of suicide. Knowing that suicidal ideation often stems from feelings of hopelessness and lack of any future orientation, teachers encourage students to create Hope Baskets that they can use to remind them of positive things that are happening in their lives. The baskets contain specific, tangible reasons for living, such as pictures of loved ones; reminders of places that give pleasure, such as the beach, a favorite tree, or a hiking trail; and symbols of hopes for the future, such as a college brochure, a driver's license application, or a business card in a chosen profession (Haley & Hughes, 2010). On days when a student seems particularly discouraged or depressed, staff members use the basket's contents to remind the student of the positive things in his or her life.

Collaborative partnerships with community mental health services provide emergency treatment, supervision, and support for high-risk cases. Working closely with staff and students, therapists help teens develop safety plans to use between sessions. These are written documents listing the following:

- Environmental triggers
- Agreed-upon response to triggers
- Internal coping mechanisms
- External coping mechanisms
  - ➤ Speak with a friend
  - ➤ Tell someone
  - ➤ Clinical contact: therapist, on-call clinician, ER

This level of coordination between school and clinical services provides seamless programming for teens. Staff members are able to use similar interventions throughout the school day to help teens manage their symptoms and find new hope for a future that they can control.

## IMPLICATIONS FOR EDUCATIONAL REFORM

Implicit in the current knowledge of adolescent development is the need for secondary schools to attend to the development of students' regulatory behaviors and executive functioning. Schools need to tap into teens' curiosity and encourage their participation in activities that expand their interests. Instruction that moves beyond rote learning and takes advantage of the brain's neuroplasticity can expand adolescents' capacity for higher-order thinking and abstraction.

| WHAT ADMINISTRATORS CAN DO |
| --- |
| 1. Provide extracurricular activities that encourage adolescents to explore their interests in STEM subjects, literature, art, music, and physical education. |

2. Provide students with opportunities to debate ideas, engage in mock trials, and get involved in political and environmental affairs as ways of strengthening the neural circuits in their prefrontal cortex.

3. Provide professional development training for teachers on how to recognize behaviors of students who are at high risk for suicide.

4. Enter into fiscal agreements with community mental health agencies to provide emergency treatment and support for students perceived to be at high risk for suicide.

---

### What Teachers Can Do

1. Use examples from literature and social studies to model ways of accepting past adversity and constructing a more positive and capable self-definition for the future.

2. Use homeroom class meetings or daily advisory periods to teach students how to communicate clearly and develop their ability to resolve conflicts.

3. Model ways of showing interest in others, how to celebrate their successes, and how to show support during difficult times.

4. Use role-playing to teach students the importance of aligning words with facial expressions and body language.

5. Foster teens' cognitive flexibility by integrating divergent thinking strategies into content instruction.

6. Help students increase their capacity for sequential thought through the use of stylized routines, transitional rituals, and tight adherence to the scheduling of school and classroom events.

## CONCLUSION

Adolescence marks a period of heightened brain plasticity and growth. The complementary processes of synaptic pruning and myelination increase neural connectivity and prepare the brain for the complexities of adulthood. Changes in the neocortex improve adolescents' executive functioning, social cognition, and capacity for abstract thought. The period, however, is not without its risks, especially for teens who have trauma histories. Mental illness, social isolation, and suicidal ideation can derail health development and trigger long-term problems.

CHAPTER 4

# Re-Traumatization on the Streets

Of pain you could wish only one thing: that it should stop. . . .
In the face of pain there are no heroes.

—George Orwell

The lowered self-esteem, learned helplessness, and cognitive distortions that characterize adolescents with early trauma histories increase their vulnerability to victimization by nonfamily members (Finkelhor & Dziuba-Leatherman, 1994; Latsch, Netl, & Humbelin, 2016). Teens 14–17 have more exposure than younger children to physical assaults, sexual victimizations, and exposure to community violence (Finkelhor, Turner, Ormrod, & Hamby, 2011). Many youth are victimized more than once. These polyvictimized youth risk losing fundamental capacities for normal development, successful learning, or a productive adulthood as a result of their experiences (Pickens et al., 2016).

This chapter reviews the types of adolescent victimization, the likelihood of victimized teens' involvement with the juvenile justice system, and the relationship between trauma and substance abuse. Proactive approaches to prevent the all-too-common negative effects of adolescent victimization on adult quality of life are presented.

## TYPES OF ADOLESCENT VICTIMIZATION

Traumatic experiences in adolescence often occur within the context of poverty, discrimination, and marginalization (Briere & Lanktree, 2012). Some liken the experience of youth living in chronic community violence to life in an "urban war zone," where neighborhood victimization takes place within a larger context of risk (Garbarino, Kostelny, & Dubrow, 1991). Many urban teens have high ACE scores as a result of family problems that include poverty, mental illness, addiction, and domestic violence.

Faced with the threat of victimization by strangers in the community or peers in school and continued maltreatment at home, many teens fear for their safety and doubt that anyone has the ability to protect them. Chronic victimization leaves many teens anxious and afraid, leading some to resort to delinquent aggressive behaviors (sometimes involving weapons) as a way to defend themselves (Turner, Shattuck, Finkelhor, & Hamby, 2016).

## Violent Crimes

Although adolescents are often characterized as troublemakers, predators, and violent criminals, the reality is that young people age 12 to 24 suffer more violent crime than any other age group in the United States (Catalano, 2006). Although perpetrators are sometimes other peers, the higher percentage of crimes are committed by adult predators. Teenagers are twice as likely as others to be victims of violent crime. In a national survey of high school students, one in five reported being a victim of a violent crime in the past year. Youth who are poor, African American, Hispanic, or American Indian are at the highest risk of victimization. African American teenagers are, for example, five times more likely to be killed by a gun than White teenagers. American Indian teenagers are more likely than any other group to be a victim of violent crime; their risk of victimization is 49% higher than the rate for African Americans (Wordes & Nunez, 2002).

Sex trafficking is perhaps the most shocking type of crime perpetrated against teenagers. It is estimated that at least 100,000 American children every year are victims of commercial sexual exploitation (U.S. Department of Justice Child Exploitation and Obscenity Section, 2012). Runaway and homeless youth are at particularly high risk, although some trafficked teenagers continue to live at home and attend school.

## Property Crimes

Adolescents are also more likely to be victims of property crimes than adults, although they do not often report such crimes to the police. While approximately 54% of property crimes against teens occur at school, 46% occur elsewhere by a range of perpetrators (Finkelhor & Ormrod, 2000). The most common types of property crimes are theft and robbery. Theft involves stealing or damaging personal property without use of force, whereas robbery involves the use or threat of force, and is considered a violent crime.

## Victimization by Peers

Peer victimization is relatively common and represents a distinct threat to adolescent health and development. Approximately 12.4% of adolescents report violent victimization at the hands of peers. Even higher percentages report being bullied by peers (35%) or victimized by cyberbullying (15%) (Modecki, Minchin, Harbaugh, Guerra, & Runions, 2014).

Peer victimization is linked to an increased likelihood of teens' engagement in physical fights, as well as a greater likelihood that they will develop anxiety disorders and/or depression—conditions that frequently persist into adulthood (Stapinski, Bowes, Wolke, Pearson, Mahedy, Button, Lewis, & Araya, 2014). Fear and concerns for their own safety can lead adolescents to seek protection in potentially dangerous ways. Some youth seek initiation into gangs because they believe membership in these deviant social groups will shield them from further harassment. Others hope that carrying a gun or weapon will protect them.

## Continued Maltreatment at Home

Adolescent abuse and neglect by parents or parent substitutes is another type of teenage victimization that has serious consequences for youth's mental health and academic performance. Maltreatment of adolescents is often dismissed because of perceptions that teens are less harmed by it or may in fact be guilty of causing the negative treatment to occur. Regardless of this implicit bias, the National Child Abuse and Neglect Data Set (NCANDS), developed by the U.S. Department of Health and Human Services, indicates that adolescent maltreatment cases amount to approximately 25% to 45% of all substantiated cases (*Child Maltreatment*, 2014).

The re-traumatizing effects of criminal activity, peer victimization, and continued maltreatment in the home lie in the ability of these experiences to reinforce the self-doubt and sense of worthlessness that characterize the teen population. The sense of danger that results from repeated violation of personal boundaries triggers teens' dysregulated stress response. It becomes more difficult to activate their higher-order thinking skills as they regress to the survival instincts of the subcortical brain. These teens question any hope they have for a better future where they can control what happens to them. Instead, feelings of distrust and despair are reinforced.

Staff members in trauma-sensitive schools are aware of the high rates of teen victimization and are quick to pick up on behavior changes that may signal a problem. They know that adolescents often struggle with disclosing that they have been the victim of a crime for fear that telling an adult will only make things worse. Victimization triggers feelings of shame associated with earlier traumas or concern that adults will think less of them for being duped one more time. Knowing this, teachers integrate information about crimes against teens into content-area discussions or conversations about current events. This lets students know that this type of victimization is not uncommon, and that it is definitely wrong and is definitely not their fault if it happens to them. Opening the lines of communication in this manner lets teens know that staff members are available to listen if and when they choose to disclose when a crime has been committed against them.

## FROM VICTIM TO OFFENDER

Trauma exposure among offenders is closely linked to their criminal behavior. Over 90% of male juvenile offenders experience acute and/or chronic trauma, whereas sexual abuse is the primary predictor of girls' entry into the juvenile justice system (Epstein, 2015).

Teens with a report of maltreatment that is first investigated after age 14 (adolescence-limited maltreatment) are significantly more likely to be incarcerated than those who had a first report of maltreatment in early childhood. Maltreatment experienced in adolescence has detrimental outcomes for offending that exceed those of childhood-only maltreatment, and is more closely related to delinquent behavior (Smith, Ireland, & Thornberry, 2005).

### The Relationship Between Trauma and Delinquency

Anda and his colleagues (2006) suggest that the occurrence of a "veiled cascade of events" identifies trauma as a single unifying explanation for countless forms of dysfunction, including delinquency (p. 8). The detrimental effects of repetitive childhood trauma and chronic stress on developing neural networks and the neuroendocrine systems that regulate them triggers a state of physiological and psychological alarm. Overwhelming distress and terror inhibit the ability of the brain's executive functions to mediate thought, emotion, or behavior. If the trauma persists unabated over time, this heightened state of alarm exhausts the mind's and body's resources, leaving the youth with a depleted ability to regulate affect, a rigid cognitive style, and a limited repertoire of coping strategies. These problems limit teens' ability to acquire age-appropriate self-respect, self- regulation, and interpersonal trust (Latsch, Netl, & Humbelin, 2016; van der Kolk, 2014).

The loss of personal integrity and control that results from traumatic victimization is a profound assault to the development of the self. Although the exact trajectory from polyvictimization to delinquency remains unclear, it appears that some type of emotional numbing is involved (Lansford et al., 2006). Youth distance themselves from conscious awareness of distress in a manner that increases their likelihood of acting it out in maladaptive ways.

Some teens engage in "survival coping" as a way of protesting the injustice of their maltreatment and regaining some sense of control (Ford, Chapman, Mack, & Pearson, 2006). They outwardly express defiance and callousness toward others to mask inner hopelessness, shame, and despair. If the environment does not respond to this muffled cry for help, defiance gives way to desperation. Teens resort to "victim coping," which justifies taking any means possible to avoid revictimization. This involves an increasing loss of empathy toward others, distorted interpersonal cognitions, lack of impulse control and self-regulatory capacity, and diminished sense of future.

## The Effects of the School-to-Prison Pipeline on Delinquency

The zero-tolerance policies that fuel the school-to-prison pipeline represent an extreme form of the punishment paradigm adopted as part of the War on Drugs in the early 1980s and later applied to schools following the Columbine shootings and passage of the Gun-Free Schools Act (Cerrone, 1999). It represents a criminalization of student misbehaviors and transfers educators' responsibility for developing students' prosocial behaviors to the criminal justice system. Increased police presence, checkpoints, and surveillance within schools have replaced more traditional, developmentally appropriate systems of behavior management. Early contact with police in schools often leads to a rise in school-based arrests and sets students on a path of alienation, suspensions, expulsions, and court involvement in managing disruptive behaviors–behaviors that otherwise would have landed them in the principal's office, and that could easily have trauma at their root.

Youth of color appear to be most vulnerable to the consequences of school policing. Though girls of color represent 8% of public school enrollment, they represent 14% of students receiving one or more suspensions per year. The suspensions are often the result of student resource officers (SROs) punishing girls of color for behaviors that appear to be intentional troublemaking but are actually rooted in trauma (Epstein, 2016). African American boys receive more out-of-school suspensions and expulsions than White students, and over 70% of the students involved in school-related arrests or referred to law enforcement are Hispanic or Black (Blad & Harwin, 2017).

## Restorative Justice

Restorative justice is a philosophical framework that can be applied in a variety of contexts: the justice system, schools, families, communities, and others. Unlike coercive punishment, restorative practices create a brain state of relaxed alertness that enhances adolescents' ability to think creatively and learn.

Historically, most criminal justice systems emphasize retribution and punishment as the consequences of transgressions by offenders against victims of crime (Maiese, 2004). Restorative justice approaches shift away from punishment and retribution, particularly for young offenders and for less serious offenses, and toward creating the conditions that allow for restoring relationships and making things right.

The switch from viewing delinquency in terms of offenders and vic-tims to identifying harm that may have been done to everyone involved is an enormous one. Trauma-sensitive schools favor a restorative approach to discipline that is grounded in the relationships between students and the adults who collaborate with them in their development. Misbehaviors are addressed in a manner that strengthens these relationships, rather than alien-ating or coercing the wrongdoer.

When students return from an absence as a result of incarceration, sus-pension, or expulsion, they participate in reentry circles. They are welcomed back into the school community and reminded of past contributions they made to support other students. With support and guidance from other circle participants, the returning student makes a plan to repair any damage his or her past behaviors may have caused. Restitution is focused less on punish-ment than on repairing the harm done to others by the offending behavior and resolving not to engage in it again.

Engaging adolescents in restorative discipline practices involves training them to use the skills needed to address misbehavior and conflict resolu-tion in an empathic and nonjudgmental manner. These include delivering affective statements, asking effective questions, and actively listening to what others have to say.

Advisory meetings provide a comfortable setting in which to model the collaboration and respect needed to practice restorative discipline. Role-plays with scripted dialogue are used to teach teens these new ways of com-municating with one another. With enough practice, youth come to see the effects of their behavior on the entire classroom community. When they make a positive contribution, everyone celebrates. When they misbehave or engage in destructive conflict, they learn that their actions affect every-one. But because they are a team, peers support wrongdoers' efforts to make amends and quickly reintegrate them into the group for their own benefit and for that of the whole classroom community (Sprague, 2014).

The collaborative problem solving that is at the heart of restorative disci-pline is practiced within parameters that ensure adolescents' emotional safe-ty. Some classrooms use "respect agreements" (Claassen & Claassen, 2008), while others use "t-charts" that list what respect looks like and sounds like (Johnson & Johnson, 1990). Within this protective context, youth become more aware of the thoughts and feelings of others. The ensuing dialogue increases their tolerance of differences. They acquire the cognitive flexibility needed to explore alternative explanations of events and situations in a non-judgmental manner.

Classroom practices that foster restorative discipline include a desk con-figuration that encourages teamwork, a peace table at which students can meet to resolve differences, flexible grouping, and opportunities to work on projects that encourage perspective taking and negotiation. Some teachers find training in peer mediation helpful in implementing restorative discipline techniques, while others prefer short check-in and check-out times at the beginning and end of each class. Whatever techniques are selected, the goal is always the same: to teach adolescents that relationships can be repaired and old wounds healed when the goal is restoration rather than punishment.

## TRAUMA AS A GATEWAY DRUG

Rates of alcohol and drug use increase dramatically between the ages of 12 and 18. Lifetime rates indicate that 73% of youth have used alcohol and 48% have used illicit drugs by their senior year of high school (Squeglia, Jacobus, & Tapert, 2010). Although not all teens who abuse alcohol or drugs have trauma histories, there is a strong correlation between substance abuse and trauma in adolescents. Though one in five teens between the ages of 12 and 17 engages in abusive/dependent or problematic use of illicit drugs or alcohol each year, the rate is three times higher among those with trauma histories (National Child Traumatic Stress Network, 2008). The close relationship between trauma histories and substance use appears to be linked to teens' attempts to manage the emotional dysregulation, heightened arousal, and sense of hopelessness resulting from trauma. The dangers involved in adolescents' attempts at self-medication include detrimental effects on neurodevelopment and cognition, an increase in dangerous risk-taking behaviors, and a high likelihood of addiction (Hughes, McElnay, & Fleming, 2001).

## Effects of Substance Use on Neurodevelopment and Cognition

Adolescence substance abuse is associated with alterations in brain structure, function, and neurocognition. Structurally, alcohol use increases the risk of neurodegeneration (degeneration of the nervous system, especially of neurons) in the hippocampus and changes in white matter maturation (Zeigler et al., 2005).

*Hippocampus.* The hippocampus is an area of the brain associated with memory and learning. Hippocampal volume is smaller among teens who use alcohol than in their nondrinking peers (De Bellis, Clark, & Beers, 2000). Reduced volume in the hippocampus is associated with poorer performance on recall and retrieval tasks, with teen drinkers performing 10% lower on information recall than nondrinking peers (Zeigler et al., 2005). Alcohol consumption also appears to have an indirect effect on working memory by decreasing teens' visual-spatial skills. Alcohol consumption compromises their ability to visually encode images, and maintain and manipulate them in their mind. Likewise, deficiencies in this area impact adolescents' ability to use rehearsal strategies to practice new behaviors in their mind (Guerri & Pascual, 2010).

*White Matter Maturation.* Heavy drinking in adolescence causes damage to the frontal regions of the brain (Crews, Braun, Hoplight, Switzer, & Knapp, 2000). It is linked to alterations in the white matter of the frontal lobe, including a reduction in the number and thickness of white matter tracts (Vargas, Bengston, Gilpin, Whitcomb, & Richardson, 2014).

Alcohol consumption also appears to trigger microstructural changes in the corpus callosum, the massive collection of white matter that connects the right and left hemispheres of the brain. These may help explain why teens who drink are less capable of efficiently transferring information across hemispheres than their nondrinking peers.

In addition to these structural changes, alcohol interferes with brain functions such as perception, executive functioning, spatial operations, and attention—all of which are important to academic performance and future functioning (Brown, Tapert, Granholm, & Delis, 2000; Giancola, Shoal, & Mezzich, 2001; Tapert, Aarons, Sedlar, & Brown, 2001; Tapert & Brown, 1999). Alcohol further exacerbates the problems teens have with correctly perceiving others' intentions. Its consumption is also linked to poor problem solving, difficulty generalizing information, and a reduced capacity for abstract thinking (Zeigler et al., 2005). Together, the structural alterations and neurocognitive deficits that result from teen drinking have implications for adolescents' intellectual development that can continue to affect them into adulthood.

## Effects of Substance Use on Dangerous Risk-Taking Behaviors

Although adolescence is the healthiest period of life, overall morbidity and mortality rates increase 200% between middle childhood and late adolescence/early adulthood (U.S. Department of Health and Human Services, 2007). Alcohol frequently plays a role in these adverse outcomes. Regardless of adolescents' initial motivation for using substances, alcohol or drug consumption is inevitably linked to risky behaviors that can have traumatic consequences for themselves and others. Even adolescents who are not generally considered "frequent risk takers" engage in more risks when under the influence of alcohol. Alcohol use among youth increases their risk of re-traumatization and polyvictimization. It is strongly correlated with violence, risky sexual behavior, and other harmful behaviors (Hingson & Kenkel, 2004).

*Violence.* Heavy alcohol and poly–drug use increase the likelihood of aggressive behaviors as well as vulnerability to victimization in both male and female teenagers. This relationship persists even after controlling for other variables such as home environment, grade in school, and race. Teens who drink may be more at risk of violence because of reduced physical coordination and poor decisionmaking in threatening situations (Shepherd, 2006).

*Risky Sexual Behavior.* Sexual violence and unplanned and unprotected sexual activity constitute yet another set of alcohol-related problems. Adolescents are more vulnerable to experiencing (or committing) sexual assault when drinking, as well as more likely to engage in risky sexual behavior. Early onset of alcohol use has also been associated with unplanned and unprotected sex. A college survey conducted by the Boston University School of Public Health showed that among drinkers, those who had their first drink before the age of 13 were twice as likely to have unplanned sex and more than twice as likely to have unprotected sex (Hingson & Kenkel, 2004).

## Effects on the Likelihood of Adult Addiction

A history of early trauma increases the risk of developing a substance abuse disorder or addiction that can continue throughout the life span. Adolescents who start to drink before the age of 15 are four times more likely to meet criteria for alcohol dependence at some point in their lives (Grant & Dawson, 1997). Early alcohol use is associated not only with more regular and higher levels of alcohol use and dependence in adulthood, but also with serious mental health and social problems, including diminished work capacity and, in some cases, premature death (McCambridge, McAlaney, & Rowe, 2011).

Teens who meet the criteria for posttraumatic stress disorder (PTSD) and engage in underage drinking appear to have a greater risk for substance abuse disorder or addiction. Adolescents with PTSD have dangerously high levels of the stress hormone cortisol. This can destroy neurons in the brain, interfere with emotional regulation, and limit their ability to successfully engage in daily life. These individuals often have very high anxiety levels. They often reexperience traumatic events, avoid circumstances that trigger trauma memories, and suffer from hyperarousal (NIMH, 2016).

Adolescents who experience PTSD begin using alcohol as a way of self-medicating, hoping it will alleviate these symptoms. Unfortunately, drinking can actually worsen the symptoms of PTSD, including the anger and irritability, emotional numbness, and social isolation typically associated with the disorder. Over one-quarter of teens with PTSD who drink to relieve symptoms develop a substance use disorder that can continue into adulthood (National Child Traumatic Stress Network [NCTSN], 2008).

Alcohol abuse prevention programs and recovery support rank high among the services offered in trauma-sensitive secondary schools. Staff members collaborate with community mental health services to provide students with a full range of recovery services. The intensity of support varies, but often includes a recovery homeroom or a dedicated chemical dependency counselor. Students in recovery are blended with students not in recovery for most, if not all, of the school day. The emphasis that trauma-sensitive schools place on connection and helping students pursue self-soothing activities offers additional supports for sobriety.

Student assistance groups modeled after Twelve-Step programs meet regularly, using peer support to help youth recognize their problems and stay sober. The times of the meetings are staggered so that students can spread their absences over their entire schedule of classes, rather than miss one class repeatedly. Members are encouraged to take personal responsibility for their problems and their recovery, within the supportive context of fellow students who are also struggling with substance abuse disorders.

## IMPLICTIONS FOR EDUCATIONAL REFORM

Given the prevalence of trauma among the school population, there is a critical need for secondary schools to adopt a more trauma-sensitive approach to discipline and student engagement. As more states address ways of approaching poor academic and social outcomes through a trauma-sensitive lens, evidence of the effectiveness of these methods continues to grow (McInerney & McKlindon, 2014). Evidence includes decreases in rates of suspensions and expulsions, increases in student attendance, and an increase in the percentage of students who meet or exceed benchmark targets in math and writing (Stevens, 2012).

Adoption of a trauma-sensitive approach holds the promise of interrupting the trajectory of traumatized teens heading toward delinquency and substance abuse disorders, as they learn new skills to regain control of their lives.

---

**WHAT ADMINISTRATORS CAN DO**

1. Implement use of an evidence-based antibullying program such as the Olweus Bullying Prevention Program (http://www.violencepreventionworks.org/public/index.page) throughout the school.
2. Provide professional development on restorative discipline as part of a schoolwide commitment to implementing this behavior management framework.
3. Offer a restorative justice class that students can take as an elective.
4. Establish a restorative justice youth leadership group.
5. Develop the staff's capacity to share power with students.

---

**WHAT TEACHERS CAN DO**

1. Integrate information about crimes against teens into content-area discussions or conversations about current events.

2. Teach students the difference between peer conflicts and bullying.
3. Provide students with direct instruction on conflict resolution and mediation skills.
4. Encourage teens to use apps like ZenView and Breathe2Relax to manage daily classroom stress.
5. Link classroom learning to viable 21st-century career opportunities.
6. Treat students returning from juvenile detention centers as teens who committed a crime rather than as criminals.

## CONCLUSION

Contrary to popular belief, adolescents are more likely to be victimized than any other age group in the United States. Yet their victimization at home, in the community, or at school is minimized because of perceptions that its effects on teens are less harmful or the suspicion that youth are at fault and deserve the negative treatment they receive. This implicit bias toward teen culpability can eventually lead to patterns of victim coping by which youth justify taking any means possible to avoid re-victimization. Until schools and communities are willing to recognize the inner hopelessness, shame, and despair that underlies teen defiance, the lives of too many of America's children will continue to be lost to the criminal justice system and mind-numbing substance abuse disorders.

CHAPTER 5

# The Neurobiology of Interdependence

The nature of this flower is to bloom. Rebellious. Living. . . .
Blooming gloriously for itself.

—Alice Walker

Adolescence is a period of increased social engagement marked by teens' transition from the familiarity of their home to the uncertainty of relationships with others with whom they have no formal ties. It involves the development of a coherent sense of self capable of reorganizing existing relationships with caregivers and initiating new relationships, primarily with peers.

The reorganization of existing relationships involves transcending internalized representations of caregivers and establishing a sense of self that is distinct and individuated. This process of self-individuation represents a period of great possibility for teens with early trauma histories. With the right support, it enables them to release negative perceptions of themselves as shameful or deficient and work to establish a positive self-image capable of moving beyond past adversity.

This chapter presents an overview of how traumatized teens are able to move beyond a history of insecure or ambivalent early attachments toward a life of earned secure attachments to peers and chosen partners. Emphasis is placed on the effects of trauma on early attachment and self-individuation, how attachment patterns influence behavior, and how neuroplasticity facilitates the development of social interdependence.

## ATTACHMENT, INDIVIDUATION, AND TRAUMA

Bruce Perry (2013) defines the attachment process as the "emotional glue" needed for future relationships. Self-individuation as well as the capacity and desire to relate to others depends on the organization and functioning of specific parts of the brain that develop in this process. It requires caregiver attunement to an infant's changing needs, coupled with the ability to match the child's affect, attention, and gestures. Mirroring infants' vocalizations and movements reinforces the sense of connection between the caregiver and child. When both infant and caregiver attend to the same object or event, the sense of reciprocity and shared intention between them is strengthened. These episodes of joint attention start with the caregiver following the infant's eye gaze. The two then engage in a conversation about what the baby is looking at. The willingness of the caregiver to pick up on the infant's interest, labeling and describing it, contributes to the child's language development and sense of personal agency (Ainsworth, 1964).

Attachment patterns develop as caregivers help children construct the explanatory narrative that defines their experience and begins the process of individuation or self-definition. The way children remember the events of their lives impacts their ability to cope with present and future stressors. The structure and content of parent-guided reminiscence reflects the caregiver's own coping skills and attachment status. Secure attachment results when children sense that the caregiver is available and competent, the self is worthy of care, and the world is safe and secure. It requires a high degree of caregiver attunement to the nonverbal expressions of the infant's arousal and affective state. Caregivers are able to appraise and respond to the child's needs, regulate them, and communicate them back to the infant as manageable and under control (Fosha, 2003).

Secure attachment relationships are characterized by an interactive synchronicity that helps parent and child maintain a level of positive arousal that encourages curiosity and learning. Reliance on the caregiver as a secure base enables children to physically explore their environment, knowing they can return to the safety of their caregiver's presence. With enough repetition, a sense of security is firmly established. Even when miscues or misunderstandings occur, the caregiver can regulate the infant's negative state by repairing the misunderstanding in a timely manner.

Trauma and neglect mar the attachment relationship in ways that make it difficult for caregivers to provide children with this type of coregulation. The inability of caregivers to provide timely and consistent feedback to children results in a pattern of insecure attachment. As a result, children lack a sense of internal control, also referred to as personal agency. Powerless in the face of their caregivers' unpredictability, they create explanatory narratives characterized by feelings of helplessness and despair. They are unable to set future goals or try new roles. They show little interest in learning new things.

## Attachment Patterns and Neuroplasticity

Brain plasticity refers to the brain's necessary capacity to change as a result of input from the environment. Brain circuits are built in a bottom-up sequence over the course of the developmental period between infancy and age 5. The brain is most plastic during the early period of development, meaning that during this time it is the most vulnerable to the effects of attachment failures that threaten neural development. As brain circuits stabilize, they become increasingly difficult to alter. The window of opportunity for neuroplasticity is 0–5 years because of the synaptic (strength of connection between brain cells) and cellular (number of brain cell connections or synapses) changes that occur during that period. Neuronal connections develop in a use-dependent manner (see Figure 5.1). The more often they are used, the stronger they become. In infancy, the brain is making 700 connections per second, more than at any other period of life (National Scientific Council on the Developing Child, 2007).

This rapid growth in early childhood has both a positive and a negative side. The positive side is that young children's brains are primed to benefit from enriching, developmentally appropriate learning environments. The negative side is that this openness to learning makes young brains more vulnerable to developmental problems in impoverished or threatening environments. However, because cellular development is use-dependent, children are capable of recovery if they are given intense early intervention that repairs the attachment relationship so that more positive neuronal connections can be made.

Adolescents who experienced attachment failures in their early relationships can learn to draw comfort and support from teachers and others they encounter later in life, provided that their patterns of insecurity are recognized and responded to in a manner that repairs early damage. Teens manifest the results of early childhood trauma in two extreme ways: They either resist adult engagement in a manner that seems sullen and remote, or they attach too readily, clinging to anyone who displays even the slightest attention to them (Schuengel, Oosterman, & Sterkenburg, 2009). Teachers need to be especially mindful of students who demonstrate an apparent lack of interest in them. It is all too common for adults to respond to uninterested youth with in-kind behaviors. This further inhibits any interest the students may have in others. What these students need instead is sustained contact with adults who show an unwavering interest in them. This can increase their ability to respond to another's efforts to engage them, which in turn helps sustain their curiosity and ability to learn.

Although many teens with attachment issues avoid contact with others, some display what is referred to as "indiscriminant proximity seeking" (Schuengel, Oosterman, & Sterkenburg, 2009). These youth bond too easily with anyone who shows a passing interest in them. This puts them at risk for maltreatment by peers, as well as adult predators who recognize their vulnerability. These students benefit from collaborative relationships with adults who are able to set and maintain appropriate boundaries.

## Right Hemisphere Development

Attachment relationships shape the unconscious self-system of the brain's right hemisphere (see Figure 5.2). This evolves in the preverbal stages of

Figure 5.1. Expanded Neural Connectivity

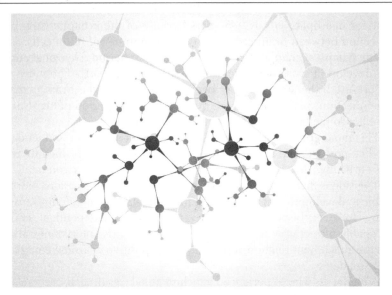

Figure 5.2. Limbic Areas of Right Hemisphere

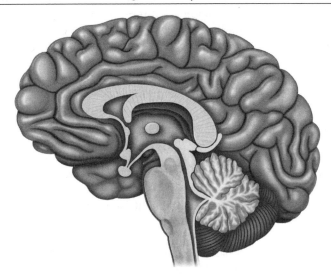

development. The impact these relationships have on the cortical and limbic autonomic right cerebral hemisphere involve far more than the fundamental sense of safety and security usually associated with it (Schore & Schore, 2008).

These relationships shape the preverbal matrix of one's core sense of self that evolves into the dynamic unconsciousness (Schore & Schore, 2008). This nonverbal self-definition unconsciously guides the individual in interpersonal contexts throughout life. The encoded strategies of affective regulation learned in infancy become the building blocks of children's self-regulation.

Because of the essentially collaborative nature of the attachment process, when caregivers themselves have trauma histories, their own disorganized, insecure attachment patterns are affectively burned into the infant's developing right brain (Schore, 2001, 2003). Caregivers' inappropriate or rejecting responses to the infant's needs induce traumatic states of enduring negative affect in the infant. These interfere with the development of the arousal-regulating process. Instead of playing a modulating role in helping the infant manage his or her internal needs, the caregiver either induces an extremely high level of stimulation and arousal, as in the case of abuse, or extremely low levels, as in the case of neglect.

Trauma has the unfortunate effect of leaving its victims in the past, unable to move forward (van der Kolk, 2014). Instead, experiences in the present trigger the sensations and feelings of past traumas over which they had no control. The result is that even in adolescence, students with early trauma histories can be thrown back into their past and compulsively reenact earlier events.

When traumatized teens experience violent emotions, their minds are often incapable of matching their frightening experiences with reassuring cognitive schemas. Their recollections of past traumatic experiences and emotions remain embedded within the right hemisphere, influencing behavior although lacking the language necessary to explain or articulate them (Bloom & Farragher, 2013). The memories remain split off from consciousness and voluntary control. When triggered, they result in extreme, inexplicable, and overwhelming emotional arousal. This reaction is caused by partial or complete loss of the normal integration between memories of the past, awareness of the self in real time, and immediate sensations and control of bodily movement.

## Individuation and the Emergent Self

The development of a coherent sense of self depends to a large extent on children's opportunities to explore their environments and develop internalized speech or self-talk. In secure attachment relationships, children are curious about their surroundings and investigate things they are attracted to under the loving supervision of attentive caregivers. Age-appropriate independence in early childhood enables children to develop personal interests and self-confidence in their ability to respond to new situations. They learn to independently participate in familiar activities, knowing they can rely on others when help is needed (McElhaney, Allen, Stephenson, & Hare, 2009).

Caregivers who encourage children's exploration of their environment frequently engage them in conversations about what they are doing. They reminisce about things they enjoyed doing or people they were happy to see. They help children anticipate what's happening in the near future and what preparations need to be made. They use words to talk about the child's behavior, and make suggestions if necessary about how to change what they are doing to be more successful in achieving their goals. With enough practice, children eventually continue this dialogue with themselves, using it to monitor their behavior and prepare for upcoming events.

Traumatic experiences establish a false dichotomy in children's early attachment relationships between safety and exploration. Uncertainty about the caregiver's behavior toward them affects the degree to which they can express their emotions or needs without fear of reprisal. They are uncomfortable with separation and question their ability to set goals or express interests of their own.

Caregivers who are incapable of forming secure attachments seldom engage children in the ongoing collaboration required for the development of internal language. As a result, children who lack secure attachment are impulsive and generally lack strong self-monitoring skills. Their limited exposure to meaningful conversations with adults results in depressed vocabulary scores, while memories of their "unnarrated past" produces an incoherent and confused sense of self (Bloom & Farragher, 2011, p. 113).

Individuation during adolescence parallels young children's exploration of their environment and the development of internalized speech. Adolescents can function more independently than they did as children, and many have at least some ability to use self-talk to monitor their behavior. The emotional support, guidance, and affection of caring adults is, however, still critical to their adaptive development, particularly with respect to autonomy. Caregiver support helps adolescents engage in autonomous exploration of themselves and their environment. It enables them to direct their attention to the important social and emotional development tasks of forming friendships and romantic relationships and regulating their behavior and emotions (McElhaney et al., 2009).

Classroom strategies such as polling and other informal queries about youth's preferences for simple things like their taste in music or preferred types of physical activity give students additional opportunities to define who they are in a safe and playful manner. Each time teachers or peers reference a teen's personal preference, they provide feedback that strengthens self-definition. Repeated often enough, this feedback enables adolescents to construct a self-image that includes self-regulatory monitoring of their behavior.

## ATTACHMENT AND BEHAVIOR

Adolescents' early attachment relationships predict the trajectory of their future ability to get along with others and have positive social interactions. Teens with secure attachment histories have the confidence and problem-solving skills needed to meet the academic and social demands of school. Those with insecure attachment patterns are inclined to behave in ways that are less confident and sometimes self-defeating. Problems associated with poor self-regulation, depression, and risk-taking behaviors are common throughout adolescence. Some teens behave aggressively, while others are anxious and easily frustrated. In either case, they need reparative experiences that help them move beyond their early attachment failures (Siegel, 2012; Wallin, 2007).

## Arousal/Self-Regulation

Self-regulation requires adolescents to have the ability to monitor their behavior and adjust it to meet the expectations of the environment around them. It involves reflection and the ability to use self-comforting strategies to keep internal arousal at a manageable level. Some teens find that physical activities such as running or strength training elevate their mood and help them relax. Others find that listening to music or physical proximity to a trusted friend calms them down and helps them unwind. Acquiring this skill necessitates collaboration with caring adults who are more concerned about understanding students' internal states than they are about enforcing disciplinary rules. An adult's willingness to help teens gain insights into how to regulate their internal states is an important resource for students who missed out on opportunities to coregulate with their first caregivers. It helps them move toward more independence and control.

Collaborative models of discipline mark a notable shift away from more traditional paradigms such as Lemov's Taxonomy (Lemov, 2010), "broken window theory" (Wilson & Kelling, 1982), or the federal government's policy of "zero-tolerance" (Noguera, 1995). These existing models require immediate, often coercive, consequences for noncompliant behaviors without any investigation into the teen's motivation. Each time these policies are enforced, teachers and school administrators miss an opportunity to partner with adolescents and help them tap into their cerebral cortex or higher brain to regulate their level of arousal. In fact, these disciplinary policies reinforce the reactive survival mechanism of the lower brain and prevent the teenager from moving forward.

## Depression

Depression is a common mental health problem among adolescents. In teens with trauma histories, it is frequently comorbid (meaning occurring simultaneously) with posttraumatic stress disorder (PTSD)—a condition characterized by nightmares, flashbacks, hyperarousal, avoidance of trauma reminders, and numbing (Gerson & Rappaport, 2013). Irritability, angry outbursts, and poor concentration are often observed among depressed youth with or without PTSD symptoms. Adolescents with trauma histories also have more severe suicidal ideation, more suicide attempts, and more frequent self-injurious behaviors than non-traumatized peers (Lipschitz, Winegar, Nicolaou, et al., 1999).

Staff members working in trauma-sensitive schools often collaborate with mental health professionals to identify and eliminate trauma triggers experienced by their students, develop appropriate coping skills that can help teens manage their stress, and arrange for necessary clinical interventions to relieve symptoms of depression and PTSD. At school, emphasis is placed on ensuring students' safety and encouraging them to have positive attitudes toward themselves and others. Depressed youth often have an attentional bias toward the negative things in their life. They see their stresses and problems more often and more clearly than they see their successes and opportunities for joy. They are more likely to display anxiety or avoidance behaviors such as arriving late to class or failing to complete assignments in a timely manner. They need more reassurance than their peers and more opportunities to practice the art of positive thinking.

Helping adolescents acquire a more optimistic outlook requires collaborating with them to expand their explanatory narrative to include a sense of personal agency, as well as the ability to imagine a future. Overcoming a pervasive sense of pessimism is never easy. It involves engaging youth in a manner that helps strengthen their prefrontal cortex through repeated opportunities to set goals, make choices about goal-related behaviors, and evaluate the efficacy of their choices.

Depressed teens also benefit from classroom environments where teachers encourage students to notice and acknowledge one another's positive attributes. These activities serve a reparative function for teens who need to develop greater self-awareness, while at the same time fostering a climate of belonging and respect.

## Risk-Taking Behaviors

Risk-taking behaviors peak during adolescence (Steinberg, 2014). Traditional theories attribute this to changes in the dopamine circuit in the brain, heightened reactivity to stress, and a cognitive style characterized by hyperrational thinking (Siegel, 2013b).

*Changes in the Dopamine Circuit.* Adolescence ushers in dramatic changes in the chemistry of the brain's reward system (Steinberg, 2014). The baseline secretion of dopamine, the neurotransmitter responsible for good feelings and pleasure, is lower during adolescence than in either childhood or adulthood (Siegel, 2013b). As explained in Chapter 3, changes in dopamine levels explain teenagers' behavior and motivation, particularly their desire for pleasure-seeking activities even when those activities involve risks. Additionally, the high experienced when dopamine is released is greater during adolescence than at any other period of life. This is especially true in the presence of peers, who appear to heighten the intensity of these rewarding feelings. As Siegel explains, "the ordinary becomes extraordinary," thus encouraging teens to seek out exciting, pleasurable experiences regardless of the risks involved (Siegel, 2013a).

*Reactivity to Stress.* A growing body of research suggests that adolescents are particularly vulnerable to the disruptive effects of prolonged stress (Romeo, 2013). This is partly because of adolescents' sensitivity to their environment and partly because of their hormonal reactivity. Teens' filters for stimuli coming in from the environment are weak, and their reaction to the hormone THP further compromises their ability to manage stress. Unlike THP's ability to reduce anxiety in children and adults, it has the opposite effect on teens, making them more anxious in stressful situations (Jensen & Nutt, 2015). The uneven development of limbic areas in the brain that govern appetitive drives, reward, and novelty seeking, and the prefrontal cortex's cognitive control system, further complicates the situation. Until the prefrontal cortex "catches up" with the limbic system, reactive responses to stress dominate teen decisionmaking and increase the likelihood of risk-taking behaviors.

Stress reactivity contributes to adolescents' vulnerability to neuropsychological dysfunctions, including anxiety and depression. Efforts to control the discomfort associated with these may explain their involvement in risky behaviors related to drug and alcohol abuse (Simons, Whitbeck, Conger, & Conger, 1991).

*Hyperrational Thinking.* Teens evaluate the pros and cons of risk-taking behaviors in a manner quite different from that of children or adults (Siegel, 2013a). Children and adults weigh the pros and cons of a behavior in a manner that considers possible negative effects as a reason to avoid doing something, even if the probability of a harmful outcome is low. Adolescents take a different approach. The potentially positive effects of a behavior outweigh any probability of danger. They believe that they can avoid any potentially undesirable consequence of the behavior. Teens' tendency to minimize the potential danger of risky behaviors excuses participation in activities that justify their need for excitement despite the risks involved. This pattern of rationalization, combined with immature executive functioning, limits their ability to inhibit their attraction to behaviors that other age groups choose to avoid.

## ATTACHMENT AND SOCIAL INTERDEPENDENCE

By adolescence, youth develop an internal representation or working model of attachment that guides their interpretation of interpersonal transactions with others and affects the quality of their new relationships (Bretherton & Munholland, 1999; Cassidy, 2001). It is a period of great potential for teens with trauma histories, provided they have access to environments that enable them to find meaning in their past experiences and decide what role these will play in their future going forward. The ability to integrate personal trauma into a temporal sequence of past, present, and future provides teens with the autonomy they need to access the degree to which childhood experiences are still affecting them and determine what they want to do about changing such effects.

Teachers can work with the brain's neuroplasticity to support teens' efforts to integrate past traumas into a more complete personal narrative that enables them to engage in interdependent adult relationships. This occurs when teacher–student collaboration avoids new traumatic exposure while fostering protective factors that facilitate the development of adolescent mindsight and empathy. As  mindsight, or the capacity to attend to one's internal world, increases, so does empathic understanding of the internal world of others. Potentially maladaptive patterns of adult attachment that are the result of early attachment failures can be reframed in these relationships. Caring adults work with teens to help them *earn* the capacity for secure attachment in future relationships.

## Reducing New Traumatic Exposure

The quality of adolescents' early caregiving experiences produce one of two relational systems—high-quality relationships produce a social system for bonding and getting close, while less adequate care results in a hierarchical system characterized by rules for keeping your distance and knowing your place (Hughes & Baylin, 2012). High-quality caregiving experiences result in bonded relationships that facilitate the development of five interacting neural systems that increase youths' understanding of themselves and others. These include the social approach system that allows teens to approach others without becoming defensive; the social reward system that makes interactions enjoyable; the people-reading systems that helps adolescents interpret nonverbal communication and predict what others may do next; the meaning-making system that helps them make sense of their social world; and the executive system that regulates interpersonal conflict and maintains a balance between prosocial and defensive behaviors (Hughes & Baylin, 2012).

Less-than-adequate care shifts the dynamic between parent and child from a bonding relational system to the creation of a social hierarchy relational system characterized by power-based ranking relationships. Teens raised in social hierarchy relational systems are less in tune with themselves and others, and have fewer ways of resolving conflicts.

Unfortunately, public secondary schools often opt for behavior management techniques and discipline policies that reinforce the social hierarchy relational system. The school structures and teachers don't present opportunities to attach (Bergin & Bergin, 2009). When events at school reinforce past negative experiences, they do nothing to reduce the effects of trauma in students' lives. Adolescents with early trauma histories continue to perceive adults as untrustworthy and the world as unfair. They are unable to overcome past attachment failures that limit their academic and social mastery.

Staff in trauma-sensitive schools know that for many teens, early care experiences cause them to expect hierarchical relational systems. For this reason, teachers avoid classroom management techniques that are authoritarian or harsh in nature. Instead, they use a combination of brain-based strategies, such as playfulness, acceptance, curiosity, and empathy, to "surprise" students' mistrusting brains by challenging their expectations of adult behavior (Hughes & Baylin, 2012). This is the first step in building collaborative relationships that prevent the triggering of old traumas. As bonds between teachers and students develop, youth eventually generalize a feeling of attachment to their school. Adolescents who feel bonded to their school feel a sense of belonging, knowing that "the people in my school like me" (Bergin & Bergin, 2009).

## Enhancing Protective Factors

School experiences help adolescents compensate for early attachment failures by providing them with a protective environment designed to reshape their perceptions of themselves and others. In addition to buffering the effects of insecure attachment on teens' achievement, high-quality relationships with teachers can inspire students to have a higher opinion of themselves (O'Connor & McCartney, 2007). This occurs when high expectations for performance and behavior are paired with the scaffolds and accommodations that youth need to achieve them.

Student–teacher collaboration provides an excellent framework for modeling problem-solving strategies, including the need for persistence and optimism when faced with obstacles in meeting a desired goal. This type of collaborative relationship helps adolescents learn to generate alternative solutions to challenging situations. With enough practice, they are able to achieve the cognitive flexibility needed to negotiate the demands of everyday life.

Opportunities such as peer tutoring or working on community outreach projects like food and clothing drives teach teenagers how to care for others and participate with peers to achieve a common purpose. These experiences are particularly valuable when adults take the time to acknowledge the teens' involvement and let youth know how their contributions benefit others. Adult survivors of childhood trauma are quick to note that assuming a caregiving role toward others helped them overcome early adversity.

## ADULT PATTERNS OF ATTACHMENT

Working models of attachment behaviors show some continuity from childhood to adulthood (Mikulincer & Shaver, 2007; Pietromonaco & Barrett, 2000). Children who transition into adolescence with secure attachment histories move into new relationships with confidence and curiosity about the future. Teens whose early attachment experiences lacked a soothing sense of reciprocity with their caregivers show signs of insecure attachment in their interactions with others. Their behaviors are similar to those in children with avoidant, ambivalent, and disorganized attachment styles.

### Avoidant Attachment

Youth with avoidant attachment behaviors protect their insecurity by minimizing their need for relationships. These adolescents appear emotionally distant and display little affect, although research shows that their internal state is in a constant state of hyperarousal (van der Kolk, 2014). While internally craving attention, they do nothing to demand it. They have difficulty seeking help from others or relying on social support. They dismiss any desire for connection to others, taking a certain pride in their ability to "go it alone." Their explanatory narrative involves a self-definition as defective or broken in some way. They fear exposure and avoid intimacy in an effort to avoid rejection.

### Ambivalent Attachment

Behaviors associated with ambivalent attachment are more dramatic. Children engaged in this type of attachment relationship are quite good a drawing attention to themselves by crying, screaming, or having tantrums. Though they seem to derive little comfort from the caregiver's proximity, they maintain an unwavering focus on him or her. As they move into adolescence, these teens are preoccupied with what others think about them and whether or not they can "hold on to" relationships with peers or potential partners. This preoccupation with the quality and security of new relationships heightens teenagers' anxiety and can inhibit their ability to explore their own interests or develop the autonomy needed to sustain interdependent relationships.

### Disorganized Attachment

Children develop a disorganized attachment style when caregivers are emotionally unavailable to them as a result of mental illness, domestic violence, or an unresolved traumatic past. They face the untenable situation of needing the caregiver for survival but being unable to attract his or her attention. This has a shattering effect on the attachment process that leaves children terrified of their caregiver and others who assume a similar role. Lacking any sense of internal security, these children trust no one. Their explanatory narrative is marred by perceptions of themselves as deficient and ineffective. These feelings, coupled with an inability to regulate their emotions, set the stage for academic and social failure. Even as adolescents, they are prone to acting-out behaviors. They lure unsuspecting adults into "reenactments" of their original attachment failure by pushing them to a point of rejecting them or engaging in harmful behaviors that mimic those of their primary caregiver. Even as adults, they continue to struggle with creating a coherent personal narrative capable of integrating unresolved traumas into a broader context.

## Neuroplasticity and Earned Secure Attachment

The neuroplasticity of the adolescent brain offers teens the opportunity to modify the effects of early attachment failure within the context of new relationships with caring adults who can help them become more fully aware of their internal strengths. Referred to in the literature as "earned autonomy" or "earned secure attachment," this process of neural integration and reconnection is a primary goal of teachers working with students with trauma histories in that it enables these teens to make sense of their lives and move beyond the effects of past attachment failures (Main & Solomon, 1990; Siegel, 2007). Teachers collaborate with students to help them increase the reflective activity in their brains and train them to use the analytical power of the left hemisphere to manage the emotional data stored in the right hemisphere.

Experiences of insecure attachment and early trauma interfere with the integration of the left and right hemispheres (Crittenden, 1998; Kagan, 2002; Teicher, Anderson, Polcari, Anderson, & Navalta, 2002). As explained earlier, this is partly because of the effect of maltreatment on the size and volume of the corpus callosum, the band of muscle that connects the hemispheres and transmits messages between them (McCrory, De Brito, & Viding, 2011).

Helping adolescents integrate the neural circuitry of the left and right hemispheres, as well as the subcortical brain and the neocortex, is critical to their success in achieving earned secure attachment (Siegel, 1999). Although some of these integrative functions are the responsibility of the prefrontal cortex, social relationships and the narratives individuals tell about themselves and their relationships also contribute to these regulatory processes (Cozolino, 2006).

The personal narratives of youth with trauma histories are often fragmented and appear frozen in the past. The fragmentation is the result of the sensory nature of many of the teens' memories and their inability to use language to bring right hemisphere experiences into conscious awareness in the left hemisphere. Recursive rumination about previous maltreatment further undermines efforts to focus on the present or to imagine a future.

Teachers can play an important role in helping teens "revise" their personal narratives in a manner that modifies self-image, fosters flexible affect management, and increases their ability to self-soothe and problem-solve (Cozolino, 2006). Using a combination of emotional attunement and language, staff members in trauma-sensitive schools help teens learn to talk about their internal and external experiences. As youth become better able to express their thoughts and feeling in words, they learn to regulate their internal state. With enough practice, teens begin to recognize that their life is about more than their early trauma. Negative experiences of the past are integrated into a larger context, and students earn a higher level of integration and security than they thought possible because of their early attachment failures. They are able to "reclaim admission to the social world" (Cozolino, 2006, p. 325).

## IMPLCATIONS FOR EDUCATIONAL REFORM

Collaborative partnerships with adults help teens advance self-regulation by repairing the damage of earlier attachment failures. These relationships are far more beneficial to students' future success than coercive models of discipline that fail to show similar results. Alliances between mental health professionals and teachers provide additional support to teens who are struggling with symptoms of depression and posttraumatic stress disorder by identifying and removing trauma triggers. These and similar practices hold the promise of helping teens overcome past trauma and achieve earned secure attachment, an important predictor of adult well-being.

---

### WHAT ADMINISTRATORS CAN DO

1. Create a school climate that fosters collaboration and bonding rather than hierarchical relationships.
2. Provide all staff with professional development training on brain-based behavior management techniques.
3. Provide opportunities to participate in wellness programs that include workshops on stress management and relaxation techniques.
4. Create a school climate in which students have easy access to adults in supportive roles. Encourage mentoring relationships and classroom meetings, and utilize interns recruited from local graduate school programs in education, social work, and psychology to increase the number of adults capable of forming relationships with students.
5. Foster a school climate where teachers are encouraged to collaborate with students in a manner that helps them regulate their emotions and maintain a comfortable level of arousal. Developmentally appropriate pacing and level of difficulty helps children stay involved and avoid "zoning out" or feeling overwhelmed. So do frequent check-ins and movement breaks.

6. Foster a school climate that builds students' capacity for optimism through schoolwide goal setting and public acknowledgment of positive outcomes.

7. Publicly acknowledge the contributions of those who go out of their way to help make school activities a success.

8. Provide staff with professional development training concerning the nature and intensity of traumatic memories.

9. Working effectively with traumatized students requires teachers to monitor their own reactions to student behaviors in order to remain objective, especially when de-escalating volatile behavior. Provide teachers with frequent opportunities to acquire the skills needed to manage their own internal state and avoid triggering reenactments of teens' past traumas.

10. Approach students' behavior with curiosity rather than judgment. Ask, "What were you thinking when you threw that boy's sneaker on the roof?" rather than saying "Don't throw anyone's sneakers again."

11. Encourage teachers to show an unwavering and consistent interest in the students for whom they are responsible. Provide coverage so that teachers can collaborate with mental health professionals on an as-needed basis to create appropriate interventions for specific students.

12. Partner with community agencies to sponsor mentorship programs for youth who can benefit from individualized adult attention.

13. Develop and implement schoolwide expectations of adult–student interactions that foster acceptance and respect. For example, use students' names when addressing them. Encourage staff and students to greet one another when they pass in the hallways. Display artwork that celebrates diversity and inclusion.

14. Use school songs, mottos, logos, and so on to help students connect with their school as a home base where they belong.

## WHAT TEACHERS CAN DO

1. Use eye contact, interest, and gesture matching to convey respect to students and a willingness to collaborate with them.

2. Replace authoritarian classroom management techniques with brain-based strategies that build a sense of collaboration and support.

3. Hold students to high expectations for performance and behavior, paired with the scaffolds and accommodations that children need to achieve them.

4. Provide students with opportunities to care for one another through providing a needed service or support.

5. Be emotionally available to students, supporting their efforts to manage their emotions and behavior.

6. Create a classroom environment that supports a dynamic relationship among the brain, mind, and body of the students and teachers who participate in it.

7. Use observation to appraise students' inner states and support their efforts at self-regulation based on your perception.

8. Use observation and active listening to establish positive relationships with students that allow them to feel safe and free to explore.

9. Provide positive behavioral supports such as physical proximity, choices about seating, visual templates, and developmentally appropriate pacing to help students maintain a comfortable level of arousal.

10. Provide students with opportunities to strengthen their prefrontal cortex through goal setting, choice making, and self-reflection.

11. Encourage teens to notice and acknowledge one another's positive attributes.

12. Follow a consistent daily schedule to help students learn what to expect.

13. Engage students in serve-and-return exchanges to increase their understanding of reciprocal relationships. Serve-and-return interactions require adults to be sensitive to students' needs and signals and respond to them in a manner that sustains or extends the interaction.

14. Provide students with opportunities to explore their interests through enrichment activities that broaden their experience and expose them to alternative ways of imagining a future.

## CONCLUSION

Students' attachment relationships affect every aspect of development. Secure attachments encourage adolescents to explore new skills and areas of interest. Patterns of insecure attachment have the opposite effect. Various types of experiences alter the neural architecture of the brain in ways that limit teens' ability to trust themselves or others. Positive attachment relationships with teachers help students compensate for early attachment failures. Positive experiences in school give them the confidence they need to explore new concepts and behavior. Within this protective environment, students are able to reshape their perceptions of themselves and others. With enough support, they achieve earned secure attachment.

# CHAPTER 6

# The Teacher's Role in Trauma-Sensitive Schools

> To do well [in school], especially for students who expect and dread failure, is to know sharp delight.
>
> —Nicholas Hobbs

The teacher's role in a trauma-sensitive school is to integrate what is now known about adolescents' neurodevelopment into classroom practice. Access to neurologically informed best practices is an important step in helping students overcome trauma-related challenges. Primary emphasis is placed on instructional design, implementation of a tiered system of support for students' self-regulation, and collaborative partnerships with teens that provide them with the coaching they need to make good choices and avoid self-destructive behaviors. Teachers don't have to mention trauma to be trauma-sensitive. They do have to engage adolescents in noncoercive ways. The use of threats or authoritarian expectations is likely to trigger the "fight, flight, or freeze" reaction in traumatized teens and limit their ability to learn.

This chapter presents an in-depth discussion of two instructional designs that are particularly advantageous to adolescents with trauma histories. Both emphasize teachers' use of ongoing formative assessment, which helps teens acquire the self-awareness they lack as a result of early traumatizing experiences. A tiered intervention model for use within a trauma-sensitive school is described, as well as the benefits of collaborative teacher–student partnerships. Strategies for using these partnerships to buffer stress, prevent reenactments, and foster personal agency are provided.

## DESIGNING TRAUMA-SENSITIVE INSTRUCTION

Instructional design in a trauma-sensitive school makes use of current research on adolescent neurodevelopment. Ongoing formative assessment helps teachers differentiate instruction in a manner that is responsive to students' needs and preferences. Teachers then work with the brain's plasticity to optimize teens' capacity for higher-order thinking and executive functioning.

## Neurodevelopment and Instructional Best Practices

Magnetic resonance imaging (MRI) provides important insights into the neural processes that organize adolescents' cognition. These data provide a framework for teachers to develop and sustain classroom environments that work with the brain's plasticity or adaptability to enhance youth's development. These enriching practices begin with the teacher's ability to foster positive relationships and extend to both the physical aspects and emotional tone of the learning environment.

There is no question that teachers can offer teens the opportunity to reverse earlier attachment failures. To be successful in this role, teachers need to be knowledgeable about how the attachment process works and capable of understanding the emotions that result in disruptive or hostile behaviors. Equipped with these competencies, teachers can collaborate with adolescents to help them acquire the control they need to regulate their feelings and behaviors.

Teachers are most successful with traumatized youth when they are able to establish themselves as a source of comfort and a secure base for exploration and learning. They establish this sense of connection by creating a relationship that reflects a balance of support and opportunity. They build teens' self-esteem by holding them to high expectations while providing the necessary scaffolds to guarantee success. The focus is on cultivating a sense of well-being and competence through repeated experiences of acceptance and care (Green, 2014). With enough support, youth learn how to navigate around obstacles and display adequate persistence in the face of difficulty.

As teens begin to experience academic success, it is important for teachers to recognize their role as "brain builders." Committed to using neuroplasticity to help students achieve their highest potential, teachers set clear goals about the higher-order thinking skills they want teens to acquire. They then design instructional activities that expose students to an appropriate level of neurodevelopmental demand, with scaffolding provided as needed.

This neurodevelopmental model of instruction reflects two important shifts in teacher performance. The first involves expanding the focus of ongoing assessment to include an evaluation of the power of particular activities to achieve neurodevelopmental goals. The second consists of differentiating instruction in a manner that allows students to meet content expectations using a variety of processing skills: auditory, visual, and motor.

Adolescents build their capacity for higher-order thinking and cognitive control within safe, comfortable environments. Protection from outside threats nourishes the brain's inherent curiosity. Within this context, the teacher's role is transformational, expanding youth's dendrite mass by helping them make new connections to prior knowledge. As indicated in Figure 6.1, dendrites are the branched projections of neurons that transfer information to another. The greater a student's dendrite mass, the more efficient a learner they become.

Figure 6.1. Dendrite Mass

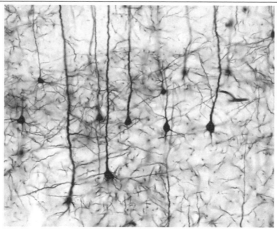

Neural networks are strengthened through the use of an instructional format that gives students frequent opportunities to do something with what they are learning–talk about it with a peer, complete a hands-on activity, create a model symbolizing what they have learned. "Think-pair-share," PowerPoint presentations, and interactive note-taking are familiar strategies that can be used to provide opportunities for immediate reinforcement. Each facilitates storage in long-term memory, helping to "cement" the new information onto existing neural structures.

## Customizing Instruction

Trauma-sensitive schools differentiate instruction using the principles of universal design for learning (UDL). First developed to ensure equal access for children with disabilities, these principles emphasize the need to design instruction in a manner that is flexible enough that it can be customized and adjusted to meet individual needs. Consideration is given to the three primary neural networks associated with learning: the *recognition network*, which is the "what" of learning; the *strategic network*, which is the "how" of learning; and the *affective network*, which the "why" of learning (CAST, 2011). Assuming that learning differences exist in any group, instruction is designed in such a manner that there are multiple routes of access to each network.

*Recognition Network.* The *recognition network* consists of the mechanisms by which teens gather facts and categorize them. When the same information and content are available in multiple modalities, students tend to select the one with which they are most comfortable. This increases the speed with which they can recognize patterns and efficiently categorize new information.

Adolescents with early trauma histories share the need for presentation of material in multiple modalities. They also require accommodations to the unique characteristics of their language processing. These include their tendency to focus on the relational aspects of language. Traumatized teens often miss important information or content because they pay more attention to the teacher's face and body language than what is being said. They struggle with spontaneous speech and have difficulty responding to direct questions. They are more likely to participate when teachers provide a "wait time" between when a question is asked and when a response is expected, or when small groups work together to come up with an answer. When teachers are aware of the effects of trauma, they differentiate the "what" of instruction in a manner that includes accommodations to these distinct learning characteristics.

*Strategic Network.* The *strategic network* relies heavily on students' executive functioning and development of the prefrontal cortex, a lengthy process that continues throughout adolescence. Until this development is complete, the teenage brain relies on the temporal lobe, the parietal lobe, and the amygdala for language and decisionmaking (Wolfe, 2010). As a result, teens are prone to making decisions based on feelings rather than logical thought.

Early adversity only heightens the impulsivity and reactive style that characterizes adolescence. Teens with trauma histories use a trial-and-error approach to learning as opposed to one that involves planning and self-reflection. They are youth who "act and then think" (van der Kolk, 2001) and give up easily in the face of new or challenging tasks.

Teachers build teens' capacity to think strategically when they provide explicit instruction on executive functions and help students integrate new information into related patterns of prior knowledge. Concept maps and encouragement to summarize and symbolize new learning in an alternative format, like the arts or writing across the curriculum, helps teens consolidate new information in long-term memory (Willis, 2011).

Explicit instruction on higher-level executive functions occurs through teacher–student collaboration that builds teens' capacity to understand basic concepts, underscoring organization and higher-order thinking. Early trauma and/or attachment failures interfere with teenagers' understanding of sequence, prediction and estimation, and time. Traumatized youth experience events as random, uncontrollable, and outside time. They need help understanding the relationship between effort and outcome. They live in the moment and find it difficult to project a future where they can control what happens to them.

Meaningful supports include teacher modeling of goal-setting behaviors, as well as teaming with students as they create plans to meet personal goals. Explicit feedback is provided in a timely, informative manner, and students have time to reflect on their progress and performance. Consistent implementation of this type of assistance helps strengthen the prefrontal cortex, making adolescents' executive functioning more effective and automatic.

**Affective Network.** The *affective network* involves knowing how to attract teens' attention, engage their interests, and sustain their effort. It is a neural network that relies on teachers' willingness to engage youth in an ongoing dialogue about how to design instruction in a manner that is both interesting to teens and capable of sustaining their attention and effort. Together, ongoing formative assessments of both the purpose and process of instruction, as well its outcomes, create a dynamic feedback loop between teachers and students in which both have a voice. Stagnant repetition of one-size-fits-all lesson plans is replaced with plans that reflect the unique experiences of one teacher and one group of students.

Such close collaboration with teachers is very conducive to helping adolescents with early trauma histories learn. For perhaps the first time, teens know that an adult is interested in them and willing to change to accommodate their needs.

This sense of connection places teachers in a unique position to help traumatized adolescents. It helps teens replace their innate sense of despair with optimism about their future. This change of perspective is strengthened each time teachers provide students with opportunities to learn about who they are and what they are capable of doing. Examples include giving teenagers positive feedback about their personal attributes, such as offering to help a classmate catch up with her or his work. Specific praise about the effort students expend working on difficult tasks makes youth more aware of their capacity for persistence and effortful control. Choice making is another way to foster this process of self-differentiation, especially when time is spent discussing whether the choices students make help them achieve personal goals. Staff in trauma-sensitive schools encourage teens to make choices about how specific learning or behavioral objectives will be met; what tools will be used; and what, if any, support will be needed. Encouraging this level of autonomy increases classroom safety by giving students a voice in decisions that affect their lives (Green, 2014).

Safety is further enhanced by use of predictable classroom routines, calendars, charts, and visual timers that help students know what to do and how to do it. Alerts and previews prepare teens for changes in activities or schedule and help them anticipate what might happen during unusual or novel events.

Even within the context of a safe learning environment, adolescents with early trauma histories require sustained apprenticeships to acquire age-appropriate self-regulatory behaviors. As they become more aware of their reactivity and internal state, continued support is needed to develop adaptive strategies for managing and directing their emotional states. These strategies typically center on coping with the anxiety caused by external triggers or internal rumination about events over which they have no control. Once acquired, the strategies allow teenagers to direct their attention to classroom instruction and stay involved.

## Dialogic Teaching

Dialogic teaching uses the power of conversation and dialogue to extend adolescents' thinking and increase their understanding of things they are learning. Students are introduced to different types of conversations or "talk" that are used in different environments and for different purposes: talk for everyday life, learning talk, teaching talk, and language used for classroom organization. Each type of language adheres to principles that promote collaborative, reciprocal relationships. In trauma-sensitive schools, there is an explanation for the fact that "teacher talk" is often sprinkled with indirect requests that are meant to be obeyed—for example, "Would you please open your book and turn to page 20?" A distinction is made between a "teacher talk" request and similar indirect requests used in everyday talk, which do involve actual choice, as in "Would you like to take a walk with me?" Teens learn that this is not the case when these questions are posed within a classroom context.

Students with early trauma histories are often deprived of language-rich home environments. Their parents spend little time talking to them. They do not engage in conversations about ideas. Time is not devoted to helping teens articulate their opinions or share hopes and dreams for the future.

Dialogic teaching provides new opportunities for youth to explore how language can be used to explore other people's ideas. This helps students expand their ability to use representational thought, a skill that is critical to the development of both empathy and inferential comprehension (Johnston, 2012).

Another benefit of dialogic teaching is its use of questions that invite students to create new stories about themselves. The teacher's question "How did you . . . ?" helps teens link their actions to positive outcomes for themselves and others. With enough practice, adolescents are able to rewrite their explanatory narrative.

### IMPLEMENTATION OF A TIERED SYSTEM OF SUPPORT

The tiered approach to intervention employed in trauma-sensitive schools is unlike traditional service-delivery models that require either special education eligibility and/or psychiatric diagnosis. Instead, trauma-sensitive schools rely on a public health model that uses risk assessment to determine needed supports. Risk factors such as poverty, recent life adjustments, Adverse Childhood Experiences or ACEs, trauma history, and emotional and/or behavioral concerns determine the type and intensity of the supports provided. Approximately 85% of students function well with the support provided at Tier 1. Supports at Tier 1 are universal in nature and reflect sustained implementation of educational best practices, such as instruction at students' readiness level, positive behavioral supports, and use of developmentally appropriate pacing of instruction. The remaining 15% may need more targeted or intense Tier 2 and Tier 3 interventions. Tier 2 support is usually provided in an additional, smaller class addressing the skill areas in which students need additional instruction. Interventions are provided by either a classroom teacher or an educational specialist who is knowledgeable in the area(s) where additional support is required. Tier 2 interventions typically target social skills, organizational skills, or stress management techniques. Tier 3 support is typically provided in an area outside the classroom by an educational specialist other than a classroom teacher. The ratio is 1:1 or 1:2 and intervention occurs daily for a short period of time. Tier 3 assistance is sometimes needed for adolescents who are trying to manage an emotional crisis such as the death of a parent or a foster care placement. Any teen can access the support available at each tier, depending on the student's life circumstances or instructional needs at any given time.

## Tiered Interventions and the Hierarchical Development of the Brain

Use of tiered interventions provides trauma-sensitive schools with a flexible framework in which to help students regulate their own arousal by relating to them where they are developmentally and reasoning with them at that level. Movement between tiers occurs as teens' circumstances change or as they become more capable of monitoring their behavior and regulating their emotions.

As adolescents mature, they increase the frequency with which they use higher-functioning areas of the brain to solve problems and work through frustration. Trauma alters this developing capacity by causing higher than normal levels of activity in the lower brain (brainstem and midbrain) (see Figure 6.2).

As a result, adolescents with trauma histories have more difficulty using their higher brain to moderate reactive responses or inhibit impulsive or aggressive behavior (Perry, 1997).

*Tier 1 Interventions.* Tier 1 interventions are traditionally referred to as universal supports that permeate the school climate (Sugai et al., 2000). They reflect expectations agreed upon by school staff and ensure that all students have access to a safe and caring learning environment. Because trauma-sensitive schools recognize that at any given time approximately 40% of the student population may have trauma histories, they are careful to anticipate unpredictable changes in student mood or behavior. Universal supports

Figure 6.2. Brainstem and Midbrain

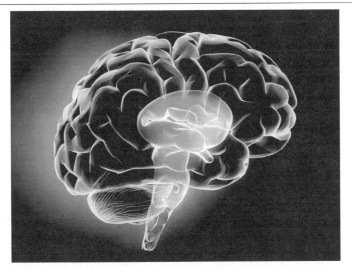

include staff members who are capable of taking over when youth's coping skills are inadequate to meet the presenting challenge or frustration. Examples include increasing a teacher's physical proximity in a manner that conveys comfort or support, redirecting a teen's attention away from a frustrating task to something more pleasurable, or giving students ample time to transition from one activity to another.

The goal of Tier 1 interventions is to provide adolescents with direct instruction on competencies associated with good mental health. These include self-awareness, self-management, social awareness, relationship skills, and responsible problem solving (Collaborative for Academic, Social, and Emotional Learning [CASEL], 2004). Opportunities to learn and practice these skills are integrated into all curriculum areas, as well schoolwide activities and celebrations that build a sense of community and belonging. Many of the interventions at this tier rely on teens' ability to access areas of higher cortical functioning and language. For example, at the beginning of class, teachers may ask students to set a personal goal that they hope to achieve by the end of the instructional block. The lesson ends with students assessing their progress toward their goals.

Expectations are adjusted to accommodate to individual differences. For example, students who are unable to function in highly verbal, cooperative groups practice required skills in a smaller group of one or two students and an adult coach.

Adolescents' capacity to function successfully with Tier 1 support is closely monitored. They are referred for supplemental Tier 2 interventions when universal screening or teacher observations indicate that they are not making adequate progress with only Tier 1 support.

*Tier 2 Interventions.* In a trauma-sensitive school, Tier 2 interventions are designed to reduce adolescents' level of arousal to pre-trauma levels of cognitive processing, executive functioning, behavior, and performance. Emphasis is placed on interventions that soothe the limbic or emotional area of the brain, while restoring teens' ability to participate in bonding relationships with adults. This capacity is often diminished by attachment failures in early childhood. Poor caregiving shifts the dynamics of the adult–child relationship from bonding to power-based competition. Interactions lack the safety one expects in early primary relationships. Teens with these types of early childhood experience continue to have a sense of powerlessness even within what should be a protective environment. These feelings trigger defensive reactions, including an increase in stress hormones and an automatic distrust of caregivers and teachers.

Tier 2 interventions usually occur in a small-group setting facilitated by teams of teachers and mental health workers, who engage participants in ways that "surprise" adolescents' mistrusting brains by violating their expectations of caregiving behaviors (Hughes & Baylin, 2012). Music and movement are integrated into group sessions that follow predictable routines and stress the self-soothing aspect of self-regulation. Some teens find that deep breathing calms them down. Other teens find that yoga relaxes them in a manner that helps them focus on their work and become more efficient. Many chair yoga poses can be integrated into classroom activities with a minimum amount of disruption.

Interventions are designed to provide adolescents with opportunities to explore the brain's interacting social systems, while at the same time learning how to collaborate safely with adults. Team leaders use a combination of playfulness, acceptance, curiosity, and empathy to (1) engage teens in conversations about what it means to have a social brain, (2) teach skills students can use to understand others, (3) help teens resolve conflict, and (4) aid youth in developing strategies for enjoying and trusting the company of others (Hughes & Baylin, 2012). They may, for example, use role-playing to explore the emotions of others or they may use trust-building exercises such as trust walks, where one student is blindfolded and has to trust the other to get them both safely to their destination.

Interventions at this level are reparative in nature. The goal is to stabilize or regulate teens' arousal to the point where they can participate in social and academic activities relying only on Tier 1 supports.

*Tier 3 Interventions.* Tier 3 interventions are the most intense in terms of frequency and duration. Whereas Tier 2 interventions help adolescents stabilize their ability to self-regulate, Tier 3 interventions help them achieve initial control of self-regulation. Students who require this level of intervention experience such over-activity in the brain stem area of their brain that their efforts to modulate impulsive or aggressive behaviors are continually thwarted.

Interventions at this level are typically one to one. The goal is to re-create the circadian rhythm, or internal regulation of body states, typically learned in infancy through coregulating experiences with caregivers. Interventions include short, repetitive, predictable, and patterned interactions; rhythmic movement; drumming; attempts at sustained eye contact; and joint attention. These are usually provided by an educational specialist with special training in sensory integration or cognitive behavioral therapy. In the case of sensory integration, services may be provided by an occupational therapist or music therapist. School psychologists or social workers are typically responsible for cognitive behavioral therapy.

The teacher's role in Tier 3 interventions is primarily collaborative. Teachers may be asked to accommodate to the needs of youth receiving this level of support by following the recommendations of the intervention team and monitoring students' progress when appropriate supports are in place.

## THE VALUE OF COLLABORATIVE PARTNERSHIPS WITH STUDENTS

Relationships with teachers offer adolescents a protective buffer against the effects of trauma, especially when they are attuned to the underlying emotions behind teens' behavior. This buffering effect is even more powerful when teachers intentionally engage teens in ways that promote personal agency and instill hope for the future.

### Buffering Traumatic Stress Through Collaboration

Given the prevalence of traumatic experiences among adolescents, staff members in trauma-sensitive schools anticipate the presence of at least one student with a trauma history in every classroom. This awareness allows teachers to take a proactive approach that engages teens in collaborative partnerships. Characterized by respect and mutuality, these partnerships help minimize the effects of trauma and prevent additional re-traumatization. Teachers' nonjudgmental understanding of the nature of trauma and its persistent ability to derail interactions and learning helps them anticipate unexpected outbursts and quickly restore students' sense of safety. Knowledge of the fragmented and sensory nature of traumatic memories motivates teachers to integrate sensory activities and self-soothing opportunities into instructional designs. They carefully construct conversations with students that help them rewrite their personal narratives of victimization and despair. They appreciate the timeless nature of trauma and they understand that survivors can be returned to their original feelings of terror and hopelessness when events in real time trigger their learned response. They know that willpower alone cannot overcome trauma, but that caring relationships with teachers can. So these teachers create learning environments where the emotions behind students' overt behaviors are acknowledged and responded to appropriately. This provides youth with the safety they need to cooperate with teachers, who can show them more appropriate ways to deal with unpleasant feelings. As a result, students are held to high standards but within the context of protective collaboration with supportive adults.

## Preventing Reenactments

Adolescents with early trauma histories or attachment failures are primed to mistrust adult authority figures. As a result, they often have extreme reactions to reasonable adult requests because these trigger traumatic arousal and discomfort. A mild criticism or perceived lack of a teacher's attention or understanding in real time sets off a reenactment of past terrors that students can neither understand nor explain (Farragher & Yanosy, 2005).

Knowing this, teachers in trauma-sensitive schools recognize these "bids for reenactment" when they occur. Rather than reacting to the student's negative behavior, they respond in a manner that reflects their commitment to collaborate with adolescents to overcome their past. When a student cannot break the trauma cycle him- or herself, teachers step in to offer assistance. They quickly engage the teen in a manner that interrupts the compulsive behavior and encourages a return to the current moment.

## Fostering Personal Agency

Early traumatic experiences rob adolescents of a sense of personal agency. This expresses itself in several different ways. Some teens appear unmotivated, avoiding new experiences and quickly giving up when a task becomes too challenging. Others are unable to make a choice or state an opinion, seeking acceptance by following the crowd. Regardless of the presenting behavior, these teens expect to be victimized. Some continue to fight for control, while most simply withdraw.

Helping youth rewrite their personal narrative occurs most successfully in learning environments where teachers intentionally instill a "can-do" attitude in students. They accomplish this by giving children a window into their own personal problem-solving process. For example, when an assembly is canceled, or students are not grasping a concept being taught, teachers talk out loud about how they will actively resolve the problem or overcome the apparent obstacle. They reframe the canceled assembly as a perfect opportunity to read more of a favorite book. Or they acknowledge that the instructional activities they are using are not achieving their goal and provide an alternative way of presenting the content.

By modeling an optimistic, assertive approach, teachers give teens a new, more resilient perspective on managing the circumstances of their lives. Frequent exposure to a variety of problem-solving strategies helps youth persist at difficult or challenging tasks.

Opportunities to contribute to the well-being of others help adolescents overcome the shame that characterizes their personal narratives. When teens experience themselves as valuable members of their school community, they acquire new insights about their capacity to make positive changes in their lives.

## IMPLICATIONS FOR EDUCATIONAL REFORM

Addressing the needs of traumatized adolescents requires providing teachers and school administrators with a new way of looking at youth's motivation and behavior. Most teachers are trained to manage behavior through contingency reinforcement. Even those trained in applied behavior analysis base their interventions on the assumption that with enough reinforcement, students can learn to exert cognitive control over their behavior.

These interventions are seldom effective with youth who have trauma histories. There are several reasons for this. Lack of personal agency makes it difficult for these teens to see themselves as the cause of another's behavior toward them. Erratic relationships with caregivers have taught them that rewards and punishments are more a function of the adult's mood than of the teens' own behavior. Adolescents find it difficult to impose a cortical brake on their impulses as a result of their characteristically dysregulated arousal.

Youth with trauma histories derive more benefit from a collaborative approach to behavior management. When teachers reframe negative behaviors as indicators of stress rather than defiance, teens are able to use teacher-directed relaxation techniques to calm down and soothe the more primitive parts of the brain responsible for their reflexive fight, flight, or freeze response. With supportive coaching from teachers, students learn to recognize differing levels of arousal and eventually employ self-soothing strategies to manage feelings of frustration or fear.

| WHAT ADMINISTRATORS CAN DO |
| --- |
| 1. Provide teachers with professional development training on how the attachment process works. |
| 2. Develop a schoolwide discipline plan that is informed by current research on the role that emotional dysregulation plays in youth's disruptive or hostile behaviors. |
| 3. Model de-escalation techniques and restorative discipline practices in interactions with disruptive or hostile students. |
| 4. Provide teachers with professional development training on how to work with the brain's plasticity to strengthen the prefrontal cortex and increase higher-order thinking. |

5. Provide regularly scheduled time and coverage to allow the tiered intervention team to function effectively.

6. Provide leadership in helping staff members reach consensus on the universal supports they agree to implement to support students at Tier 1.

7. Monitor implementation of agreed-upon Tier 1 interventions.

8. Demonstrate support for the tiered intervention team by frequent active participation in meetings.

9. Provide opportunities for teachers to meet with occupational therapists or school social workers who can assist them in managing the sensory aspects of trauma and reducing the number of trauma triggers throughout the day.

10. Develop schoolwide policies on behavior management that reflect brain-based research on emotional regulation and relationship repair.

11. Provide teachers with professional development on behavior management techniques that focus on emotional regulation rather than contingency reinforcement alone.

12. Work with local agencies to create opportunities for students to contribute to the well-being of others in their community.

### WHAT TEACHERS CAN DO

1. Use taxonomies of higher-order thinking skills (Anderson & Krathwohl, 2001) and neurodevelopment function (Levine, 2002) to select content-area activities that promote prefrontal cortex development.

2. Use the data from frequent formative assessments to build adolescents' awareness of themselves as learners.

3. Use flexible groups for activities that involve student collaboration to help teens gain insight into the complexity of their behavior and that of their peers.

4. Use collaborative group activities in a manner that increases the speed by which students integrate new information into existing schemas by strengthening the connective fiber (corpus callosum) between the left and right hemispheres. Examples include interactive note-taking and pairing new information with music or movement.

5. Confer with other members of the intervention team to develop Tier 2 or Tier 3 intervention plans for students requiring additional support.

6. Collaborate with tier intervention team members when appropriate to help children learn to stabilize (Tier 2) or achieve (Tier 3) psychological equilibrium or state regulation.

7. Collaborate with an occupational therapist to develop a "sensory diet" of age-appropriate activities that are suitable for classroom use. Include simple movement activities such as clapping or repositioning, as well as strategies that students can use throughout the day without being disruptive to peers or teachers.

8. Avoid personalizing adolescents' behavior. Instead, maintain an objective attitude with students that prevents reenactment of past traumas and provides the detachment needed to de-escalate behavior.

9. Create opportunities for youth to change their personal narratives by modeling a "can-do" attitude and helping them make meaningful contributions to their classroom community.

10. Provide adolescents with opportunities to support the well-being of others.

## CONCLUSION

Integrating knowledge about adolescents' neurodevelopment into classroom practice relies on teachers' consistent use of established best instructional practices. The relationship between differentiated instruction, dialogic teaching, and neurodevelopment is well established. Supported by tiered interventions that increase teens' ability to regulate their feelings and behavior, they offer teachers an effective framework for buffering the effects of trauma while increasing youth's capacity for self-efficacy.

# CHAPTER 7

# Trauma and Resilience

*Resilience requires relationships, not rugged individualism.*

—Harvard Center on the Developing Child

The National Research Council Institute of Medicine defines resilience as "patterns that protect children from adopting problem behaviors in the face of risk" (Chalk & Phillips, 1996, p. 4). Although early models of resilience view it as an almost superhuman ability to rise above adversity, today's models view it as a more accessible mindset that can be acquired by all students, given the right combination of internal and external supports (Masten & Coatsworth, 1995). In this context, the path to resilience depends on the capacity of teens' environments to help them develop their strengths, foster their natural abilities to make healthy adaptions to stress, and return to normal functioning after encountering severe or persistent trauma (Benson & Scales, 2009).

Students transitioning into adolescence from the protective shelter of secure attachment relationships and a safe community environment already possess many of the internal attributes associated with a resilient outlook. They are confident in their ability to achieve what they set out to do. They are optimistic about the future and demonstrate good coping skills. They rely less on external supports to adapt to new circumstances or increased demands on their emotional regulation than do peers from more insecure backgrounds.

Students whose early lives were more turbulent or traumatic require more external supports to arrive at a reliable level of self-efficacy. Opportunities to bond with teachers and peers, as well as the chance to discover their own competency and self-worth, help traumatized youth move beyond their past toward future achievements and success. This chapter explores how a school climate that fosters a culture of connection and positive peer relationships helps adolescents acquire the resilience they need to lead productive, happy lives.

## FOSTERING A CULTURE OF CONNECTION

Participation in a connected school community contributes to teens' resilience and sense of well-being. School communities designed to facilitate social bonding with supportive peers and adults contribute to the potential increase in neural connectivity that characterizes adolescence. A sense of connection at school not only improves academic achievement, but also decreases compromising health behaviors (Blum, 2005) and buffers the effects of negative family functioning and weak social skills (Loukas, Roalson, & Herrera, 2010). Connected youth are more satisfied with school and attend more regularly (Klem & Connell, 2004; Zullig, Huebner, & Patton, 2011).

Trauma-sensitive schools use this sense of connection in student–student, student–staff, and staff–staff relationships to help adolescents acquire a resilient mindset. Working with the brain's neuroplasticity, teachers cultivate students' internal assets, improve their self-monitoring skills, and increase their awareness of the external assets that are available to them.

## Internal Assets

Given youth's sensitivity to their environment, an inviting and congenial school climate is an invaluable resource in helping students with trauma histories master core competencies associated with resilience. The web of supportive relationships that characterize trauma-sensitive schools provides the safety that teens need to strengthen existing internal assets and take any corrective actions that are necessary to improve their social and academic success.

Collaborative partnerships between staff and students are essential to this work. Creating these relationships relies on the capacity of staff members to establish themselves as trustworthy and reliable. As explained in Chapter 6, adolescents with early trauma histories or attachment failures are primed to mistrust adult authority figures. Reasonable adult requests can trigger traumatic arousal and discomfort.

When this happens, teachers in trauma-sensitive schools quickly engage the teen in a manner that interrupts the compulsive behavior and encourages a return to the current moment. This type of intervention is particularly effective when it is paired with a nonjudgmental attitude that sees beneath presenting behaviors to the pessimism and lack of personal agency that are the effect of a traumatic past.

## Improving Self-Monitoring Skills

One of the confounding effects of trauma on adolescent development is the nonverbal nature of traumatic memories. The negative feelings associated with early trauma are stored preverbally in the right hemisphere, meaning that they are felt implicitly, without any language to name or explain them. Environmental triggers evoke a flood of negative emotion that the teen can neither understand nor label. Victims of early trauma don't know why they are so dysregulated and why their peers are not. Teaching them how the integration of the neural circuits of the subcortical and cortical areas of the brain develops and the effect this has on self-regulation offers teens a way out of the sense of helplessness that plagues their efforts to move forward.

Teachers in trauma-sensitive schools provide students with information about the many parts of their brain and teach them ways to avoid being hijacked by the subcortical limbic system (Siegel & Payne Bryson, 2012). When sensations arise that reflexively trigger fear, teens are reminded that there are resources they can draw on to avoid impulsive reactions to how they are feeling. They learn how to tap into the power of their neocortex to evaluate the situation and determine if fear is an appropriate response. Feedback from this more logical part of the brain is able to restore calm and help youth attend to what's expected of them in the present moment. Their capacity for executive functioning expands as incidences of downshifting decrease, and different areas of the brain are better equipped to function in a more coordinated manner. Teens are then able to engage in more purposeful behavior. They are no longer held captive by how their brains worked in the past. Instead, they have the freedom to allow new experiences to mold their brains in new ways. They can move on with their lives in resilient and life-affirming ways.

## External Assets

External assets are resources available in teens' environments that can support their efforts to overcome hardships and reach their potential. These include the influence of parents and one's sense of family identity, evidence of self-competency or skill, one's educational trajectory, degree of connection to peers and local community, and the ability to give to as well as take from society through employment and purposeful spending (Worsley, 2007). The number and quality of the assets available to individuals vary. Youth with trauma histories may struggle to identify viable resources available to them as they work to manage the effects of past or current adversities.

Realizing this, staff members in trauma-sensitive schools help students identify any possibilities that are within their reach. For example, some teens may lack supportive relationships with parents, but find that mentoring relationships with older adults helps them achieve the security they need for healthy self-exploration. Others may struggle with academics but find that their skill in music or sports gives them the confidence to persist at schoolwork until they succeed. Teens who have felt helpless to protect themselves or their siblings from domestic abuse achieve a renewed sense of personal agency when they are able to provide service to others in need.

Once viable options are agreed upon, teens and teachers collaborate on a personalized plan outlining how students will build upon these assets to develop a resilient mindset. Goals are set and monitored closely to ensure their successful accomplishment.

## FACILITATING POSITIVE PEER INTERACTIONS

The trauma experienced by many adolescents is not something that is suffered solely at the individual level. Many teens are also victims of the collective trauma that is the aggregate of adversity experienced by their community members and that has structural and social consequences. For example, neighborhood violence associated with racial tension affects individuals who identify as a part of that racial group, as well as those who are actual victims. Teens who are exposed to stories of firsthand trauma may develop a traumatic response similar to that of those involved. This is especially true if hearing about the traumatic event causes teens to reexperience their own previous trauma

Because non-White youth are overrepresented in economically depressed areas, they are more likely to experience collective trauma that is the result of neighborhood-level social and physical environmental stress (Schulz et al., 2008). These structural factors explain why Latino and Black teens are significantly more likely than White peers to have a murdered friend or family member (Finkelhor, Ormrod, Turner, & Hamby, 2005). Their risk of exposure to collective trauma is far greater than that of other same-aged peers.

Staff members in trauma-sensitive schools understand that overcoming the effects of collective trauma requires the creation of a positive peer culture that empowers students to assume helping roles in relation to one another (Giacobbe, Traynelis-Yurek, Powell, & Laursen, 1994). This peer helping process encourages adolescents to counter collective trauma by taking an active role in creating and maintaining safe environments and in encouraging prosocial attitudes, thinking, and behavior toward one another. Emphasis is placed on building a sense of collective efficacy among teens, raising awareness of their developing strengths, and motivating them to play an active role in their own well-being.

## Collective Efficacy

Collective efficacy is defined as the social cohesion among members of a group combined with a willingness to intervene on behalf of the common good (Sampson, Raudenbush, & Earls, 1997). Though closely related to self-efficacy, the emphasis is less on the individual and more on the degree to which a group is expected to behave in a manner that actively discourages problem behavior (Bandura, 1982). At the neighborhood level, collective efficacy is known to have a moderating effect on adolescent behavior, helping teens bounce back from incidents of violence or victimization (Jain, Buka, Subramanian, & Molnar, 2012).

Although most studies of adolescents' behavioral influence on one another focus on delinquent or deviant peer influence, proponents of positive peer culture point out that youth can also influence one another toward positively valued behaviors and away from antisocial behavior (Larson, 2000; Lerner, Fisher, & Weinberg, 2000; Smith, 2007). Within this context, youth are viewed as resources to one another as they negotiate the developmental challenges of solidifying their identity and extending their social network beyond their families. Adolescents use informal relationships with peers to explore common experiences and understand the meaning of events occurring around them.

## Awareness of Strengths

Early exposure to relational trauma inhibits the cognitive processes through which teens develop self-awareness. In typical development, children have repeated interactions that nurture preference and perspective. Over time, they come to understand that they can often affect what goes on around them, and they eventually learn to adjust or regulate their emotional reactions and behavior to meet personal goals. This sense of empowerment results in strong personal beliefs that define the self: who I am, what I have, what I like, and what I can do.

Adolescents with trauma histories are often unaware of the tenacity and strength that characterizes their ability to survive past or present adversities. Instead, their focus is on their perceived weaknesses or inherent "badness" that denies them access to the caring relationships and academic competence they observe among their peers. Staff members in trauma-sensitive schools recognize that an important first step in helping students take charge of their own lives is to reframe their personal narratives as stories of courage rather than defeat.

Recognizing teens' affinity for peers, staff members create opportunities for students to use positive peer pressure to support one another's transition from victim to survivor. Schoolwide rituals and celebrations create a sense of connection that is reinforced with frequent opportunities for peer mentoring, collaborative assignments, and opportunities to involve students in leadership roles within the school community.

Trust circles, which meet for 30 minutes a day, give teens an opportunity to work together on the shared goal of sustaining a positive influence on one another. Adult facilitators guide a discussion about topics, such as helping one another replace negative thoughts with more positive ones, learning how to have difficult conversations about risky behaviors, or supportive ways to call someone out for not participating enough. Within this web of mutually beneficial relationships, teens help one another get on track for a hopeful future.

## Active Role in Well-Being

Growing beyond the effects of early trauma requires conscious decision-making (Hann, 1992). It involves active engagement of students' executive functioning within the context of supportive adult relationships. With enough practice, teens' intentional coping efforts become automatic routines that enable them to achieve academic and social mastery. Teachers in trauma-sensitive schools assist teens in this process by first teaching them to recognize the physical sensations associated with stress, and then introducing them to coping strategies to manage those sensations.

Teens are often frightened by the rapid heartbeat, physical pain, and headaches that appear to come out of nowhere when past trauma reactions are triggered. They fear that these sensations, as well as the feelings of depression or panic that accompany them, will overwhelm them. Some may believe these reactions mean there is something wrong with them, that they are mentally ill or incapable of managing stressful situations. They need explicit instruction about these normal reactions to stress, as well as assertive approaches on how to handle them.

Building on teens' increased understanding of their physical reactions to stress, staff members in trauma-sensitive schools encourage teens to question the cognitive distortions that organize their lives (Wolinsky & Johnson, 1991). This involves helping them replace automatic habitual thinking with an intentional focus that allows them to take control of their attention. They learn how to observe their thoughts and emotions with a certain objectivity or adaptive distancing; this allows them to notice and change parts of their unconscious explanatory narrative that are limiting their ability to succeed (Thomas, Chess, Birch, Herzig, & Korn, 1963). They develop an ability to "extend their imagination out into a timeline of the future" where they can control what happens to them (Bloom & Farragher, 2011, p. 113). By building on their capacity for representational thought, this focused observation of their internal state, or mindfulness, allows teens to integrate perceptions of themselves that were denied or ignored in their early interactions with caregivers. The possibility of goodness is introduced into the narrative of badness. The possibility of competency is integrated into the narrative of helplessness. The possibility of hope is woven into the narrative of despair. Youth's attention shifts from people and things they cannot control toward self-care and the management of their own mental state and behavior.

Cognitive strategies such as affirmations and positive self-talk reassure teens about their ability to cope. Relaxation techniques and reflective activities teach them to observe their internal state and clear their minds of unnecessary concerns. Many of these strategies can be easily integrated into advisory periods and content instruction: taking a few deep breaths at the beginning of class to focus attention in the present moment, taking a few minutes to practice muscle relaxation before transitioning from whole group instruction to small-group work, or using the last few minutes of class time to reflect on what students learned or how well they progressed toward personal goals. Reflective activities include journaling, exit cards, or brainstorming a list of "big ideas" that summarizes the lesson's highlights.

## RESILIENCE AND ADVERSARIAL GROWTH

Adversarial growth refers to positive outcomes that can be derived from navigating stressful events (Linley & Joseph, 2004). Trauma-sensitive schools are committed to helping adolescents with early or current trauma histories develop the courage they need to find meaning in their adversities and investigate their options in the future. For these teens, resilience is less a matter of bouncing back and more a matter of moving forward (Tedesci, Park, & Calhoun, 1998).

Students of adversarial growth define it as both a process and an outcome of moving beyond early adversity. It involves rebuilding adolescents' assumptive world, recognizing positive personal attributes, and promoting coping strategies.

### Rebuilding Adolescents' Assumptive World

As already noted, most teens with trauma histories hold a variety of negative assumptions about themselves and others that leave them pessimistic about the possibility of change. Their internal dialogue is marred by beliefs that they are bad people who harm others. They feel isolated in their grief and lack any confidence in others' ability to help them. They experience themselves as hopelessly flawed, without any control over what happens to them. Changing the assumptions that inform their personal narrative means introducing notions of optimism, self-efficacy, and meaningful service into their daily life experiences.

In trauma-sensitive schools, teachers offer "expert companionship" to teens who are struggling to redefine themselves. This starts by connecting to students in a manner that conveys emotional availability and a willingness to challenge adolescents' assumptions about themselves. Teachers do this by discovering and articulating contradictory information about who students are, what they can achieve, and the positive contributions they can make to their school and the people around them (Tedesci et al., 1998).

### Recognizing Positive Self-Attributes

Rebuilding teens' ability to recognize their positive attributes requires helping them turn their attention toward positive experiences that are happening in real time. With repeated practice, teens rewire their brains in a manner that interrupts their persistent tendency toward negative thinking. Instead, they begin to scan their environment for positive experiences and increase their tolerance of positive emotions.

This cognitive shift has the potential to inhibit the automatic arousal triggered by negative emotions, thus enabling increased activity in the prefrontal cortex (Tugade, Frederickson, & Barrett, 2004). Expanding the lens through which students view their experience results in improved executive functioning and academic engagement. Youth are better able to infuse ordinary events with positive meaning and to practice problem-focused coping skills rather than reenacting past traumas.

Teachers use many strategies to help youth develop an optimistic outlook. Some teachers make it a point to share one good thing they heard on the news on their way to work. Others encourage students to create a mantra that they can chant as a team when faced with tough challenges. The point is to foster an optimistic, grateful spirit that resists the pull of recursive negativity, while offering hope for the future.

*Self-Efficacy.* Helping teens recognize the self-efficacy that they are capable of occurs when trusted adults encourage them to try new things they may otherwise avoid.

Teachers help youth develop confidence in their ability to try new things when they design instruction that is relevant to students' lives and encourage them to choose from a variety of high-interest activities. This type of personalized instruction increases participation while strengthening teens' self-efficacy and sense of personal agency. Some teachers maintain a sense of personal connection to students by adapting word problems so that they include the names of students, popular celebrities, historical figures, or sports heroes (Willis, 2007). Others link personalized instruction with opportunities to model persistence. They post lines from motivational coaches around their classrooms and encourage students to refer to them when tackling a difficult problem or situation: "Be like a postage stamp: stick to one thing 'til you get there!," "Use setbacks as motivation," "I think I can, I think I can. . . ."

The willingness of teachers to personally connect with teens and encourage them to recognize their positive attributes offers students new resources they can use to manage the circumstances of their lives. Coupled with frequent exposure to a variety of problem-solving strategies, teachers give students the skills and attitude to persist at difficult or challenging tasks.

## Positive Coping Strategies

Teaching adolescents ways to cope with stress strengthens their adaptive capacity for resilience. Many find that involvement in activities that benefit others elevates their mood, and help cope with difficulties that come their way. Making a positive contribution to others teaches youth that they have something to offer. This is a powerful message when traumatic experiences have instilled the belief that they were worthless or nothing but trouble (Mullinar & Hunt, 1997).

Service opportunities include volunteering in the school recycling program, serving as peer models for younger students, and engaging in outreach programs for the homeless or elderly. The only criteria are that these tasks address real needs and have benefits for the community.

Some teens respond well to an informal schedule of volunteer activities. Others need the structure and connection of a designated day or time to benefit from the intervention. In either case, as teens learn to care for others, their capacity for self-care also increases. They become confident in their ability to engage in meaningful pursuits.

Another important coping strategy is encouraging teens to find self-soothing activities with help them maintain a balanced outlook and find enjoyment in life. In trauma-sensitive schools, this often involves exploring leisure time activities such as music, sports, drama, playing strategic games, or practicing yoga or a martial art. The freedom to experiment with different activities until they find those that are relaxing and fun marks real growth in teens' recognizing their ability to manage their emotions and behavior.

## IMPLICATIONS FOR EDUCATIONAL REFORM

All adolescents have the capacity to make healthy adaptations to stress, and in extreme cases, bounce back from severe or persistent trauma. But they cannot do it alone. They need instruction that intentionally promotes the resources or assets required to develop a resilient mindset. Content-area curriculum that includes an explanation of how the neural circuits of the subcortical and cortical areas of the brain become more integrated in adolescence is one way schools can increase teens' internal assets. The more adolescents understand how their brain works, the better able they are to use that information to self-monitor and make decisions that are in their best interests. Instruction that involves peer collaboration and support gives students access to the important external assets of social connection and community. These are invaluable educational opportunities to increase the likelihood of teen resilience.

| What Administrators Can Do |
| --- |
| 1. Provide the leadership needed to create a school climate that fosters a culture of connection and positive peer relationships. |
| 2. Collaborate with community agencies to ensure that teens have access to programs and activities that encourage them to explore their interests and develop their strengths. |
| 3. Provide staff with professional development training on the effects of collective trauma on teens' sense of well-being and ability to learn. |
| 4. Foster a positive peer culture by creating opportunities to involve students in school governance, decisionmaking, and conflict resolution. |

5. Hold regularly scheduled schoolwide rituals and celebrations to foster a sense of connection among all members of the school community.

6. Support the idea of teens exerting a positive influence on one another by allocating time in the daily schedule for trust circles.

7. Make a point of publicly recognizing the contributions of individual staff members and students who make a contribution to the school's well-being.

8. Create a core of volunteer students at each grade level who are available to assist in school activities and projects on an as-needed basis. Publicly thank them for their service.

## What Teachers Can Do

1. Provide students with opportunities for deliberate practice in positively influencing peers by supporting their efforts to change negative thoughts into positive ones and to have difficult conversations with one another about risky behaviors.

2. Teach students how to use a "Personal Balance Sheet" of their positive attributes and things holding them back. The assignment can be found at http://www.dennistrittin.com/resources/PersonalBalanceSheet.pdf

3. Have the students in your advisory group keep a "Three Good Things" (Seligman, Steen, Park, & Peterson, 2005) notebook. Use it once a week to record good things that happen. Have students give each event a title and a detailed description of what happened. Have them state how the event made them feel and explain why they think the event happened (why it came to pass).

4. Integrate discussions of students' signature strengths and resilience into content areas.

5. Engage in meaning dialogues with students by writing emails about what makes life meaningful, prompted by a packet of 60 famous quotations on meaning. These quotations can be researched by students themselves, and those judged appropriate by peers can be included in the packet. Or teachers can provide a packet of quotations compiled from various books of famous sayings.

6. Summarize lessons by asking students to respond to the question "What went well today?" using either a popcorn or exit card strategy. The popcorn strategy involves the teacher calling on students offering to share one good thing from their perspective.

> The exit card strategy requires each student to complete the following statement on an index card before leaving the class. For example, "Things I think went well today are _____."
>
> 7. Include personal goal setting at the beginning of each instructional unit. Request written indicators of progress toward individual goals at the end of each lesson.
>
> 8. Have teens estimate how long it will take to complete a task. Compare the estimate with how long the task really took. Repeat until the estimates and real-time length are the same.

## CONCLUSION

Resilience is based on relationships that help students discover their inner talents and put them to use in the service of others. A school climate that fosters a culture of connection and positive peer relationships improves academic achievement, decreases compromising health behaviors, and buffers the effects of negative family functioning and weak social skills. Peer support, coupled with new insights into their own strength and tenacity, gives teens the courage they need to find meaning in their adversities and confidence in their ability to bounce back.

# CHAPTER 8

# The Effects of Secondary Trauma on Teachers' Lives

We don't see things as they are. We see things as we are.

—Anaïs Nin

As the widespread prevalence of trauma histories among school-age children and youth becomes more apparent, attention is being directed at how prolonged involvement with these children affects the professional and personal lives of teachers (Perry, 2014). Other professionals who advocate for traumatized children cite the stress associated with this work as the leading cause of turnover (Balfour & Neff, 1993). If the same is true for teachers, exposure to traumatic stress may contribute to the high rates of attrition among educators.

## SOURCES OF TEACHER STRESS

Teaching is ranked as one of the jobs with the greatest amount of stress-related health problems (Johnson, Cooper, Cartwright, Donald, Taylor, & Millet, 2005). This is understandable when one considers the extraordinary amount of emotional work teaching requires. It is unique among other human service positions in "its emphasis on establishing long-term meaningful connections with clients of the workplace (students) at a depth not found in other professions" (Klassen, Perry, & Frenzel, 2012, p. 15). Every day, teachers listen to repetitive stories of adolescent fear and adversity in an environment where there is not sufficient time for recovery (Perry, 2014). In addition, teachers work within a limited range of emotions deemed "appropriate for school," even in the face of distressing interactions with students (Hargreaves, 2000; Zapf, 2002). They cannot, for example, overreact when they are treated disrespectfully or cry when overwhelmed by the adversity in children's lives.

Student discipline and motivational problems are frequently reported as sources of teacher stress and attrition (Gibbs & Miller, 2014; Klusman, Kunter, Trautwein, Ludtke, & Baumert, 2008). This is especially true in situations where the behaviors interfere with the delivery of instruction to others (Chang, 2009).

These are areas of school behavior that are highly correlated with histories of early trauma and adversity. It is likely, therefore, that teacher stress is exacerbated by the fact that the unwanted conduct cannot be brought under control by traditional interventions such as consequences, punishment, or contingency reinforcement.

In the absence of trauma-specific training, teachers fail to recognize trauma's symptoms and lack the resources to reverse its course. When teachers come to believe that there is nothing they can do to effect changes in students' behaviors, they give up trying (Jablow, 2014).

## Effects of Teacher Turnover on Schools

Nationwide, more than 46% of teachers leave the classroom within 5 years (Ingersoll & Smith, 2003). This high rate of teacher attrition not only costs public schools in the United States more than $7 billion per year (National Commission on Teaching and America's Future, 2007), but it also has negative consequences for many aspects of the organizational structure of schools (Guin, 2004). These include class size, curriculum planning, scheduling, and staff collegiality. All of these affect schoolwide operations and may indirectly affect the quality of instruction.

High turnover affects all aspects of school climate and is detrimental to student success, especially in low-performing schools with above-average minority enrollments (Ronfeldt, Loeb, & Wyckoff, 2013). It destabilizes the learning environment and disrupts the continuity needed to build trusting relationships among teachers, students, and families. High teacher attrition negatively impacts student achievement by reducing access to experienced teachers and through the loss of the human capital needed for teachers to work together to improve instruction (Simon & Johnson, 2015).

## Viewing Teacher Stress and Attrition Through a Trauma-Sensitive Lens

Just as traditional behavior management techniques fail to address the complexities underlying the behaviors of adolescents with trauma histories, conventional explanations of teacher stress do not capture the depth of distress experienced by teachers working with this population of students. It is not unusual for these teachers to report experiencing painful emotions, intrusive images, and an overall sense of helplessness, not unlike that experienced by the students they teach (Hill, 2011). In fact, any educator who works directly with traumatized adolescents is vulnerable to these symptoms of compassion fatigue or secondary trauma (Abraham-Cook, 2012).

Compassion fatigue or secondary trauma is characterized by feelings of incompetence and emotional exhaustion. Teachers experiencing it have difficulty maintaining the level of emotional detachment needed to manage their feelings toward children whose behavior is frequently out of control.

Burnout develops over time and its origins are almost always related to organizational factors such as overloaded work schedules or a mismatch between skills and performance expectations. Compassion fatigue occurs when professionals feel there is nothing they can do to help the youth they are responsible for, no matter how much effort they expend. These feelings trigger a sense of hopelessness and can throw into question a teacher's beliefs about the meaning of life. Without intervention, teachers who suffer from compassion fatigue often increase their involvement in escape activities, chronic overeating, and drug or alcohol use (Portnoy, 2011).

To date, there are very few studies examining whether teachers' work with traumatized teenagers puts them at risk for the mental health issues observed among others in the helping professions. What is known, however, is that in comparison to other trauma professionals, teachers get very little training in recognizing symptoms of primary trauma in their students, and virtually no training in the self-care needed to prevent secondary traumatic stress. This has serious implications for their effectiveness and rates of attrition.

## THE BUFFERING EFFECTS OF TRAINING

Increasing teachers' understanding of the nature of trauma and its effects of children is an important resource in helping them manage their reactions to the experiences of the children for whom they are responsible. This awareness increases teachers' capacity to adequately respond to the social and academic needs of traumatized children, while safeguarding their own mental health and emotional functioning. Their risk of showing symptoms of compassion fatigue or secondary trauma is greatly reduced.

## The Protective Nature of Trauma-Specific Training and Preparation

Trauma-specific training is a key component of building the capacity of teachers to work with traumatized adolescents. Once they understand the biology of trauma and its effects on brain chemistry and child development, it becomes easier to master classroom strategies that are both self-protective and empathetic.

Implementation of a trauma-sensitive approach requires schools to carefully examine the assumptions staff members make about youth's misbehavior. Trauma theory views challenging behaviors as symptomatic of injuries students sustain in less-than-adequate relationships with caregivers. These behaviors are seen as less volitional or purposeful than many educators are taught to believe. This paradigm shift is a critical first step in helping teachers forge the collaborative relationships needed to help teens overcome past adversity. Viewing challenging behaviors through a trauma-sensitive lens leads to interventions directed at restoring safety or a more tolerable level of arousal, rather than trying to manage the behavior with more traditional methods.

Changes in educators' perception of teenagers' difficult behavior occur most successfully when training sessions are supported by ongoing technical assistance. Training content includes a thorough review of trauma theory and brain development, as well as information about compassion fatigue and secondary traumatic stress. Team-building exercises help staff reach consensus about schoolwide rules and expectations. This process stresses the importance of a consistent approach, while underscoring the need for buy-in by all staff.

Technical assistance activities support teachers' efforts to integrate what they are learning into classroom practice. These include small-group discussions, book clubs, observations, and one-on-one coaching sessions. Not all training topics require this level of support. Training on how to enhance best practices to accommodate the needs of traumatized youth can be integrated into other curriculum training sessions and applied at team-level planning meetings.

## The Benefit of Understanding the Teacher's Role

As mentioned in the Introduction, the initial failure of trauma research to address the educational needs of students with early trauma histories limited the role teachers were asked to play in facilitating these students' recovery. The growing recognition of trauma's effect on learning, as well the brain's capacity to restore itself with the proper interventions, justifies their greater involvement. The potential effect well-trained teachers can have on mitigating trauma's long-term effects is increasingly apparent. Initiatives such as the Healthy Environments and Response to Trauma in Schools (HEARTS) program in California (Dorado, 2008); the Teaching and Learning Policy Initiative (TLPI) in Massachusetts (Cole, O'Brien, Gadd, Ristuccia, Wallace, & Gregory, 2005); and the Compassionate School movement in Washington State (Wolpow, Jonson, Hertel, & Kincaid, 2009) are among the leaders in providing evidence for the effectiveness of trauma-sensitive instruction in changing adolescents' lives. Unlike clinicians who see clients once or twice a week, teachers have the advantage of spending several hours a day with their students. When that time is used to create relationships that are safe, intentional, and optimistic, the results can be transformational.

*Safe.* Knowing that fear dominates both the external and internal worlds of traumatized youth, teachers are on the lookout for signs that teens are downshifting into survival mode with the possibility of engaging in reactive, aggressive behaviors. They are quick to offer reassurance or direct students to self-soothing behaviors that help teens return to a more tolerable level of arousal.

Agreed-upon schoolwide rules and codes of conduct are adhered to by all staff members. This consistency protects adolescents from the stress and confusion associated with mixed messages and conflicting expectations of behavior.

Predictability is built into all aspects of the school day, including the schedule, the seating arrangements, and transitions from one activity or environment to another. When new or unusual events occur, teens have time to prepare for them and sufficient teacher support to calm any anxiety they might engender. Teachers use rituals to introduce and conclude instructional blocks. These rituals help youth create the anticipatory set they need to feel secure in their ability to do what is expected of them.

*Intentional.* Teachers in trauma-sensitive schools have an intentional mindset that informs all aspects of the classroom environment: the emotional tone, the choice of materials, and the sequence of activities that are introduced. They are teachers who can readily explain why they are doing what they are doing.

Their interactions with students are particularly purposeful. They are directed and designed to connote the teacher's willingness to help teens achieve three goals: (1) to manage intense emotions safely, (2) to learn how to use reasoning and judgment in the face of emotional arousal, and (3) to imagine a future where they control what happens to them.

Classroom discourse involves frequent opportunities for serve-and-return interactions characterized by adult sensitivity to students' needs and signals; the adults respond in a manner that sustains or extends the interaction. Opportunities to communicate with teachers in this manner restore teenagers' trust in the ability of caring adults to notice and respond to them. Invitations to make predictions, hypothesize about data, and problem-solve as a team intentionally promote youths' sense of personal agency and control.

Intentional teachers use ongoing formative assessments to monitor progress and student engagement, as well as to elicit feedback about teens' interests and concerns. Data from these assessments are used to adjust expectations, revise strategies, and incorporate student feedback into instructional designs.

*Optimistic.* As mentioned earlier, adolescents with trauma histories are stuck in the past. Their compulsive need to reenact earlier experiences robs them of their ability to project a future where they can control what happens to them. Teachers cannot rescue teenagers from traumatic pasts, but they can help their students move beyond them.

This cognitive shift has the potential to inhibit the automatic arousal triggered by negative emotions, thus enabling greater activity in the prefrontal cortex (Tugade, Fredrickson, & Barrett, 2004). Expanding the lens through which adolescents view their experience results in improved executive functioning and academic engagement. They are better able to infuse ordinary events with positive meaning and to practice problem-focused coping skills rather than reenacting past traumas.

Teachers use many strategies to help teens develop an optimistic outlook. These include using class meetings as a time to thank one another for random acts of kindness or having a "gratitude wall" where students record things for which they are grateful. Some send thank you notes to workers around the school, while others encourage youth to share their gratitude for achieving certain goals or overcoming personal challenges. The point is to foster an optimistic, grateful spirit that resists the pull of recursive negativity, while offering students hope for the future.

## Addressing the Contagious Effects of Trauma

It is important for teachers to understand how trauma affects those who work with its victims. Otherwise, they are at considerable risk of developing burnout, secondary traumatic stress, or compassion fatigue. Left unchecked, these reactions impact one's ability to provide effective instruction. Instead, teachers' behaviors begin to mirror those of the students. Feelings of fragmentation and isolation interfere with their ability to think and process information. A sense of heightened arousal makes them particularly sensitive to danger, so that even minor threats trigger strong emotional, physical, and cognitive responses. Emotionally exhausted, teachers resort to reactive or punitive responses to student behavior that eventually creates a "self-sustaining cycle of classroom disruption" (Jennings & Greenberg, 2009, p. 492).

Cultivating Awareness and Resilience in Education for Teachers (CARE) (Jennings, Snowberg, Coccia, & Greenberg, 2011) and Stress Management and Resilience Training (SMART) (Sood, Prasad, Schroeder, & Varkey, 2011) are two evidence-based models for developing teachers' social–emotional competency (Cullen, 2012). Both emphasize the benefits teachers derive from practicing mindful awareness. Often referred to as mindfulness, it involves careful regulation of practitioners' attention, self-awareness, and self-compassion. This self-monitoring enables teachers to notice their own emotional triggers and avoid reactive responses to them (Abenavoli, Jennings, Greenberg, Harris, & Katz, 2013). Instead, they are able to maintain the objectivity needed to respond in an effective, intentional manner (Roeser, Skinner, Beers, & Jennings, 2012). In this way, mindful awareness helps teachers manage their own emotions and understand how their emotional responses impact others.

In addition to mindfulness training, both programs provide training in other competency areas associated with reduced emotional reactivity and improved well-being in teachers. These include knowing how to set firm but respectful boundaries; demonstrating kind, helpful behaviors toward others; and managing conflict.

### PROMOTING TEACHER RESILIENCE

Resilience enables teachers to persist in the face of challenges. Although some personalities appear more naturally inclined toward a resilient attitude, it is a capacity for adaptation that anyone can develop. Trauma-sensitive schools support teacher resilience by increasing access to known protections against stress, minimizing known risk factors, and preparing teachers to use their relationships with students in positive, life-affirming ways.

## Components of Teacher Resiliency

Teacher resilience is perhaps best understood as a dynamic process or outcome that is the result of interactions between the teachers and their environment. Three dimensions of teacher resiliency are particularly effective in addressing the threats posed to teachers working with traumatized youth: good coping skills, self-regulation, and the knowledge that they create change in the lives of adolescents. Good coping skills help teachers maintain the professional objectivity needed to help teens gain control of their emotions and behavior without overidentifying with them, or personalizing their rejecting behaviors. Self-regulation of attention and self-awareness help teachers manage their own emotions and notice how their emotional responses impact others. Finding ways to create change in adolescents' lives restores teachers' sense of self-efficacy. Together, these three resilient practices sustain the sense of well-being needed to remain engaged and successful as educators.

*Coping Strategies.* Knowing how to cope with everyday challenges is a hallmark of teacher resiliency (Parker & Martin, 2009). This involves not only having good problem-solving skills or the ability to seek out and use social supports. It also requires a level of impartiality that allows teachers to transform even the most difficult situations into learning experiences. Teachers employ this coping mechanism whenever their instructional goals are met with student resistance. The capacity to remain objective in these situations allows teachers the flexibility they need to appraise the situation and make necessary changes (Skinner & Beers, 2016). Rather than personalizing the experience, they see it as an opportunity to gain a more accurate perception of student needs. It poses no threat to them or to the children with whom they remain engaged.

*Self-Regulation.* Self-regulation involves the ability to simultaneously monitor one's internal state while observing how what is going on in the environment is affecting it. The more aware teachers become of their physical reactions to stressful situations or emotionally charged interactions, the better they are able to interpret and account for them. This increases their ability to respond thoughtfully.

Self-regulation benefits all aspects of teaching, but is indispensable when de-escalating student behavior. It provides the internal support needed to refrain from reacting to overtly hostile or menacing conduct.

The better teachers are at regulating their emotions and behavior, the more equipped they are to anticipate the effect their words and actions may have on others. They carefully monitor their choice of words and tone of voice to ensure that they convey a sense of acceptance and connection. This enables them to bring a high degree of intentionality to their work, while avoiding the dangers of impulsive words and actions.

*Knowledge of Changes to Adolescent Lives.* Adolescents raised in healthy attachment relationships grow up expecting a certain level of give-and-take in their relationships. No one gets what they want all the time, but resilient relationships have sufficient elasticity to bounce back from misunderstandings. Members of a resilient relationship share the innate sense that "Home is the place where, when you have to go there,/ They have to take you in" (Frost, 1969, p. 34).

Youth with early trauma histories lack that sense of security. They overreact to perceived slights from peers, and indications of adult displeasure or judgment may trigger deep feelings of shame. As a result, these teens find it difficult to negotiate the social world of shifting and changing relationships. They are socially isolated from peers, who find them somewhat unlikeable and prone to social problems (Jagadeesan, 2012).

When teachers provide adolescents with the opportunity to acquire the security needed to form resilient relationships with others, they know the difference they are making in students' lives. This knowledge sustains their willingness to engage teens in partnership-building activities that help them acquire the self-confidence needed to participate in give-and-take relationships. As trust develops, students learn to manage their reactions to redirection, and finally acquire the skills they need to use their minds to manage their emotions and behavior.

## Ways Teachers Make a Difference in Adolescent Lives

In addition to building the partnerships that are fundamental to the success of teacher efforts, there are two other specific ways in which teachers can cultivate differences in the lives of their students. Teachers become expert at redirecting student behaviors and they effect changes in the adolescent mindset.

*Redirecting Behavior.* Being able to recognize and name what students are feeling is only part of what it takes to build and sustain trusting relationships with teenagers. Teachers also need to know how to redirect behavior in calm, respectful, and sometimes playful ways. This involves using strategies that communicate comfort and that validate the teacher's connection to students. It also includes reassuring teens that the relationships they share with teachers are capable of containing strong emotions. This support increases teens' ability to tolerate uncomfortable feelings and eventually become more capable of regulating them. Within this context, redirection becomes an opportunity to strengthen relationships and build teens' inner strength.

Conversations that involve students' behavior feel safer when they occur privately, with the teacher at eye level and physically close by. Listening attentively to the teenager's side of the story and using skillfully selected words to correct any distortions or misinformation helps the teacher move the situation forward. The final step is to develop a plan to repair any harm the wrongdoing may have caused and to avoid future incidents.

*Changing Adolescents' Minds.* Maintaining calm, loving connections with teenagers strengthens the regulating mindsight circuitry in their brains (Siegel, 2011). Mindsight is a type of focused attention that allows teens to see the inner working of their minds. Teachers foster this type of self-reflection by pausing a few times during class to give students a chance to check in on their thoughts and feelings. These "mini–brain breaks" help teens learn to monitor their state of mind. Mastering this practice enables them to break the cycle of traumatic reenactment by getting rid of ingrained behaviors and habitual responses. They learn to use their minds to take charge of their emotions and behavior. These mental and emotional changes are transformational at the physical level of the brain. By focusing on the inner workings of their minds, adolescents are stimulating the areas of the brain that are crucial to mental health and well-being.

## IMPLICATIONS FOR EDUCATIONAL REFORM

Though recruitment of highly qualified personnel is a hallmark of recent efforts toward educational reform, there has been little discussion of the stress associated with classroom teaching. Although seldom acknowledged, teaching requires above-average social competency and emotional regulation (Jennings & Greenberg, 2009). Many teachers are in daily contact with large numbers of traumatized youth, yet they have little or no access to the types of support that are taken for granted at mental health agencies.

Future efforts at educational reform should provide teachers with the training they need to adequately respond to the needs of traumatized students, while protecting their own emotional well-being. Access to regularly scheduled clinical supervision and stress management offers teachers the recognition and support they need to address the challenges of their chosen profession.

---

### WHAT ADMINISTRATORS CAN DO

1. Provide encouraging, specific feedback to teachers, including recognition of their contributions to the school community.
2. Provide strong, caring leadership that serves as a constant reminder of the vision of a trauma-sensitive school community.

3. Encourage teachers to regularly use interest surveys, conferencing, and other types of formative assessment to design student-driven instruction and reduce student resistance.

4. Use materials developed by the Mindsight Institute for Educators to increase teachers' ability to use mindsight. https://www.mindsightinstitute.com/

5. Provide teachers with specific feedback on how individual students benefit from their emotional availability and support.

6. Provide teachers with opportunities to collaborate with mental health professionals concerning the management of recalcitrant student behaviors.

7. Schedule opportunities for experienced teachers to mentor those who are new to the school or the profession.

8. Provide the leadership needed to promote the inclusion of trauma-sensitive training into district plans for teacher retention.

9. Schedule trauma-specific training and technical assistance sessions. Arrange for substitute teacher classroom coverage so content teachers can attend.

10. Closely monitor the fidelity with which staff implement schoolwide rules and expectations. Hold reminder meetings when necessary.

11. Use songs, mottos, contests, and so forth to integrate an optimistic outlook into the school climate.

12. Provide teachers with opportunities to develop the social–emotional competencies needed to work in a trauma-sensitive manner.

13. Practice consistency with regard to the guidelines and rules to which both students and teachers are held accountable.

14. Work as a team with teachers to follow through on stated policies and goals.

---

## What Teachers Can Do

1. Respond to student resistance with impartiality and a willingness to make the changes needed to increase or restore engagement.

2. Use self-awareness to monitor physical reactions to stressful situations and build the capacity for thoughtful reactions to students.

3. Engage students in partnership-building activities that help them acquire the self-confidence needed to participate in give-and-take relationships.

4. Keep an "efficacy journal." Get in the habit of taking 5–10 minutes to write down three examples of how your influence benefitted one or more students in your classroom that day. Review the journal when you need a resiliency boost.

5. Participate in online professional learning communities (PLC) addressing teacher stress and resiliency.

6. Avoid personalizing students' behavior. Use meditation and deep breathing to maintain needed objectivity and emotional regulation.

7. Be on the lookout for increased use of escape behaviors to manage stress.

8. Commit to reframing recalcitrant behaviors as possible symptoms of trauma exposure.

9. Commit to viewing students' challenging behaviors through a trauma-sensitive lens that allows you to support them in an empathic manner.

10. Commit to implementing agreed-upon schoolwide rules and expectations.

11. Help teens direct their attention to positive experiences that are happening in real time.

12. Use purposeful interactions with students to help them achieve emotional regulation and self-agency.

## CONCLUSION

The prevalence of trauma histories among middle school and high school students suggests that schools need to proactively prepare teachers to manage the stress others report experiencing when working with this population. Teachers' work with traumatized students puts them at risk for compassion fatigue or secondary traumatic stress. Training that helps teachers understand the contagious effects of trauma can offset some of the negative consequences. Learning to successfully engage traumatized teens builds teachers' resiliency by increasing their sense of self-efficacy. Acquiring coping strategies that increase social competence and self-regulation fosters the self-confidence teachers need for continued involvement with students living in difficult situations. Together, these skills enable teachers to maintain the optimism and hope that characterize trauma-sensitive schools.

# CHAPTER 9

# Next Steps

## Managing the Necessary Changes to School Policies and Practices

Become the change you want to see.

—Margaret Mead

The vison of trauma-sensitive schools as described here and elsewhere (Cole et al., 2005; Sporleder & Forbes, 2015; Wolpow et al., 2009) runs counter to much of the organized culture of schools as they exist today. The lack of transparency surrounding the prevalence of trauma in the lives of adolescents and the coercive and disempowering responses to teens' mental health and behavior issues create an intimidating school environment for adolescents with early or current trauma histories. As a result, the risk of traumatic reenactment is increased, as is the potential for further traumatization in the juvenile justice system.

This chapter describes some of the changes in school culture required by the adoption of a trauma-sensitive approach. Suggestions for needed administrative supports are provided, as well as strategies that administrators can use to encourage teacher buy-in. The chapter concludes with a section on action planning, both in terms of personal changes to which staff must commit and ways of linking trauma-sensitive changes to overall school improvement goals.

## CHANGING THE CULTURE OF SECONDARY SCHOOLS

A school's culture is reflected in its unspoken expectations and patterns of behavior that reflect a long tradition of shared meaning. Staff members construct this "hidden curriculum" based on common stories and symbolic gestures that they create and sustain through social interaction. The result is always part accumulated wisdom (how we do things around here) and part a set of largely unconscious assumptions, behaviors, and beliefs. Examples include assumptions about what motivates student behavior, appropriate teacher responses to infractions, and beliefs about how adolescents' life circumstances affect their academic and social mastery.

Aspects of school culture that need to be addressed and changed as schools transition to a trauma-sensitive model include the persistent denial of the role trauma plays in teens' educational failure, patterns of student engagement that inadvertently trigger the patterns of damaging repetition that characterize the original trauma, and the treatment of youth with behavior problems.

## Confronting Denial of Trauma's Role in Adolescent Educational Failure

A school's cultural norms reflect the values and beliefs that administrators and teachers hold about all aspects of the school environment. Traditionally, these are often based on intuitive theories or "folk pedagogies" about adolescents and learning, rather than science (Bruner, 1996). Although they are implicit and beyond the conscious awareness of teachers, these assumptions are powerful determinants of teachers' behavior toward teens.

A belief that teens are in some way to blame for what happens when violence or victimization occurs makes it hard for teachers to accept that adolescents' own mistakes or misjudgments are not at least partially responsible for the adversity in their lives. Similarly, the belief that youth are willful and in need of correction makes the awareness that youth's recalcitrant behavior is often a result of injuries sustained by caregivers difficult to bear. Both beliefs and the behaviors that flow from them are potential barriers to a trauma-sensitive approach unless they are recognized and resolved.

As noted in Chapter 1, the prevalence of early trauma histories in adolescents' lives is well documented. Until schools acknowledge the seriousness of this problem and commit to resolving it, the failure of other educational reform initiatives will continue. Trauma is not just a mental health problem. It is an educational problem. Left unaddressed, it derails the academic achievement of thousands of youth.

## Treatment of Adolescents with Behavior Problems

As our knowledge of the relationship between early trauma and neural development and self-regulation improves, it is clear that earlier efforts to help adolescents with challenging behaviors often missed the mark. This is particularly true for teens who are aggressive and difficult to control. When staff members lack information about effective interventions for traumatized youth, segregated placements in alternative schools or suspensions and referrals to juvenile court appear to be the only viable options. The labeling and stigma associated with these placements only exacerbate adolescents' internal experience of helplessness and despair. Separation from typical peers makes it impossible for them to learn appropriate behaviors (Kauffman & Badar, 2013), while the core issues driving their relentless dysregulation remain unresolved (Perry, 2006).

Trauma-sensitive schools resist the tendency of earlier models to segregate or exclude. Instead, they use formative assessment and tiered intervention to create a continuous feedback loop that links student needs and teacher responsiveness. Staff members are trained to notice "trauma flare-ups" and move in with additional support and comfort. Opportunities to practice self-reflection and self-monitoring occur throughout the day. Examples include modeling breath control or another stress management technique at the beginning of an instructional block.

Self-monitoring can be built into the last 5 minutes of a lesson by asking students to discuss the connections they see to their prior knowledge of the subject matter or by jotting down two or three ways they can use the content in their everyday life.

## The Reenactment Triangle

Relationships in trauma-organized systems are characterized by what's referred to as the "reenactment triangle" (Bloom & Farragher, 2013, p. 91). Applied to schools, it illustrates the shifting roles teens and teachers assume in the "rescuer-victim-persecutor" dynamic of reenactment. It is a largely unconscious process that is activated when students with early or current trauma histories either lash out against teachers in an effort to engage them as the persecutors in past traumatic experiences or place them in the untenable position of rescuing them from a past that's already happened and obviously can't be changed (Farragher & Yanosy, 2005).

Reenactment behaviors are triggered by teacher efforts at student engagement that inadvertently tap into traumatic memories. Physical proximity or using a loud voice can activate sensory reactions associated with traumatic memories. Criticism or perceived disapproval produce feelings of shame, while an authoritarian attitude or unfair consequences spark anger or rage. The intensity of these reactions often surprises even the most seasoned educators. They may feel angry at the student for the outburst or angry at themselves for not knowing how to contain it.

Staff members in trauma-sensitive schools are trained to understand the power of the reenactment triangle to pull them into repetitive interactions with youth that are "related to events that happened in the past rather than in the present" (Bloom & Farragher, 2013, p. 98). They know how to de-escalate teens' behavior, as well as how to remain detached in the face of adolescents' bids for reenactment of past traumas. Teachers recognize when students are getting stressed and are able to redirect them toward self-soothing activities that are grounded in the present and capable of helping them move forward.

## TARGETED AND NECESSARY ADMINISTRATIVE LEADERSHIP AND SUPPORT

Unlike other educational reform initiatives that require the replacement of the principal and 50% of the staff, the shift toward becoming a trauma-sensitive school does not involve this type of "turnaround" or "transformational" process. It does, however, require leaders capable of articulating and sustaining the vision of trauma-sensitive schools. Leadership should be inclusive, demonstrating a genuine interest in teachers' views and contributions. A robust collaborative partnership between administrators and staff members provides the support needed to overcome the resistance inherent in any systemic change.

### Articulating and Sustaining the Vision

The successful evolution of trauma-sensitive schools demands that administrators understand the underlying paradigm shifts. Their ability to articulate a clear vision of a trauma-informed approach helps staff remain focused and see the changes fully implemented (Simon & Johnson, 2015).

The vision of trauma-sensitive schools is a web of collaborative relationships that ensures the safety of everyone within. Trauma-sensitive schools are havens for adolescents where the wounds of the past are healed and the challenges of the future prepared for. Adults are emotionally available and willing to support teens' efforts to regulate their feelings and behavior. Personal narratives rewritten as traumatic experiences are integrated into a broader context of caring relationships and positive experiences. Frequent opportunities for self-reflection help both staff and students maintain the flexibility and courage needed to cultivate the resilience necessary to move forward.

Administrators support this vision by creating the structures needed for implementation (Borman & Dowling, 2008). These include (1) scheduling common planning time, (2) creating partnerships with local mental health agencies, (3) enabling teachers to get the coaching needed to manage children's trauma symptoms within the classroom (Spillane, Hallett, & Diamond, 2003; Warren, 2005), and (4) providing adequate coverage for teachers to actively participate in tiered intervention team meetings.

### Practicing Inclusive Leadership

The collaborative nature of trauma-sensitive schools, as well as the radical changes they demand, requires administrators to create a professional school culture that encourages collegiality and peer support. Improving teachers' "social working conditions" in this manner provides an incentive for buy-in and sustained cooperation in achieving long-term goals.

Teachers expect administrators to take the lead in setting a direction for school changes (Johnson et al., 2013). They also expect to be engaged in the process of identifying problems, exploring options, and contributing to meaningful decisions.

Implementation of any school initiative depends on the degree to which teachers commit to embedding its principles into their classroom practice. This decision is based on teachers' perceptions of the administration's willingness to listen to their ideas and engage them as partners in the change process (Bryk, Sebring, Allensworth, Luppescu, & Easton, 2010; Johnson et al., 2013). In the absence of a sense of shared ownership, change is gradual and most likely unsustainable.

## Managing Resistance to Change

Change is always met with resistance. Even when the change brings about improvement, it is difficult for people to give up familiar ways of doing things. But it's important to recognize that different levels of resistance exist. Early adapters embrace change quickly, often providing the impetus for others to get behind the new ideas. The risk-takers, though not at the forefront of the change process, enjoy taking risks and welcome the opportunity to get involved in something new. A third group, the fence-sitters, waits to see what happens before committing one way or another. If the proposed changes are successful, these people claim to have supported them from the beginning. If the innovation is a failure, they are quick to say, "I told you so." The fourth group is composed of "no way" people. They just do not change. Though only approximately 5% of any organization falls into this category, these people can derail the change process if administrators spend too much time trying to win them over.

Effective changes occur in organizations where administrators reinforce and reward the efforts and support offered by the early adapters and risk-takers. They can then attend to the needs of the "fence-sitters" until the necessary critical mass is achieved.

Making the changes required for schoolwide implementation of a trauma-sensitive school is more successful when administrators provide incentives to the groups supporting the initiative, thereby strengthening their commitment to the process. The knowledge that they have something to offer adolescents with early trauma histories is a meaningful incentive for many teachers. Others appreciate the additional training opportunities that working at a trauma-sensitive school provides.

Teachers who are "on the fence" about trauma-sensitive schools often do not feel equipped to handle the behavioral needs of students with histories of early adversity. Some of their resistance comes from a perception of themselves as lacking the skills needed to make the required changes. Others feel the new expectations expand the teacher's role beyond their comfort level.

Some administrators find that all these teachers need is the reassurance of knowing they will not be judged by the noisy or disruptive behaviors of the students assigned to them. They need to be reminded of the collaborative spirit that characterizes the trauma-sensitive approach. Teachers and administrators work as a team. They rely on one another to lend a hand with students whose behavior is difficult and offer new ideas to improve the situation. Others find giving reluctant teachers an opportunity to visit schools that are already using a trauma-sensitive approach is helpful. Teachers who are still uneasy may need continued coaching and support to develop the confidence they need to fully embrace the initiative. Most teachers come to realize that when done in a collegial manner, embedding trauma-sensitive practices into their classrooms is something they are capable of doing. They realize that all students, not just those with early trauma histories, benefit from these practices.

## CREATING AN ACTION PLAN FOR IMPLEMENTATION

The transition to a trauma-sensitive school requires broad systemic changes. Administrators and teachers often wonder where to begin. It is a given that all schools need training and technical assistance to make the shift to becoming trauma-sensitive. But individuals will most likely join the conversation at different entry points. Finding out what these points are is an important first step in developing an action plan for sustainable change.

### Personal Assessment

Achieving the goal of a trauma-sensitive school is best accomplished at the local level, where a strong commitment to inclusive leadership exists. The initial decision to introduce the required changes should, however, be made at the district level. Raising awareness of the need for trauma-sensitive schools usually takes the form of districtwide professional development. Initial training is often facilitated by outside consultants who are skilled at providing an overview of the trauma-sensitive approach and persuading participants of its benefits to students. From there, principals and local school leadership teams can create action plans that are unique to their schools.

### Action Planning Process

The action planning process starts with an assessment of what, if any, trauma-sensitive strategies are already in place at the school.

Figure 9.1 lists nine features of trauma-sensitive schools that are described here and elsewhere (Cole et al., 2005; Wolpow et al., 2009) to explain the approach. Its purpose is to identify the trauma-sensitive practices used

Figure 9.1. Components of a Trauma-Sensitive School

| Component | Exists | Somewhat Exists | Needed |
|---|---|---|---|
| Schoolwide awareness of the need for implementation of a trauma-sensitive approach | | | |
| Regularly scheduled training and coaching provided to ensure staff understanding of how to implement a trauma-sensitive approach | | | |
| Policies and procedures in place that reflect an understanding of the need for strict confidentiality concerning issues of child custody | | | |
| Web of collaborative relationships in place to ensure safety and support | | | |
| System of tiered intervention in place | | | |
| Structures in place to support implementation (co-planning time, including partnerships with local mental health agencies and coverage for tiered intervention meetings) | | | |
| Use of differentiated instructional designs capable of promoting teens' neural development | | | |
| Use of classroom management techniques that combine recommended practices from the PBIS and PPC models | | | |
| Stress management practices integrated throughout the day | | | |

by individual staff members, as well as to begin a discussion of how best to generalize implementation schoolwide.

Once an initial assessment is completed, decisions are made regarding changes required to move toward full implementation. This involves (1) determining the order in which model components are addressed, (2) developing appropriate goals and benchmarks for each component, and (3) identification of any additional resources that are required.

Changes of this magnitude do not happen quickly. Schools often decide to create 3- to 5-year implementation plans, with a separate task/timeline for each component. This approach gives schools time to firmly establish class-room changes that reflect a trauma-sensitive approach. These incremental shifts eventually become the norm and bring about permanent changes in the school culture.

## Linking Trauma-Sensitive Changes to School Improvement Goals

The changes required to implement a schoolwide trauma-sensitive approach directly affect what teachers do every day. Some of these changes involve the need to *release* values or patterns of behavior that teachers value or feel comfortable with. Teachers who rely on an authoritarian model of behavior management to bring out the best in their students may find it difficult to re-lease this belief in order to practice the more collaborative methods favored by the trauma-sensitive approach. Teachers who favor quiet classrooms may find the chatter and noise associated with student group-work discomforting.

Similarly, the shift to a trauma-sensitive approach *expands* the teacher's role to include increased responsibility for teens' emotional well-being and mental health. These changes require additional training and changes in teaching style that some may feel is more than they "signed on for."

Teachers find these role changes easier to manage if they are linked to increases in student achievement and their own job satisfaction. Integration of trauma-sensitive benchmarks into already-agreed-upon school improve-ment goals helps teachers remain committed to the change process. Cele-brating small victories such as improved class participation, less disruptive behavior, or fewer incidents of bullying is another way to encourage teachers to stay motivated. This is especially true when administrators connect these improvements with an increased use of trauma-sensitive practices.

## Monitoring Progress

Evaluation is an important element of any action plan. It helps determine if the action plan was implemented as intended and whether the anticipat-ed outcomes were achieved. Although schools can use outside evaluators to monitor progress, other less costly alternatives are an option. One that lends itself well to evaluating progress toward a schoolwide trauma-sensi-tive approach is the formation of a transition monitoring team. This team is composed of staff members working in different positions at the school. Their purpose is to (1) monitor implementation of the action plan, (2) make recommendations for changes as appropriate as a result of shifts in personnel or other unexpected circumstances, and (3) assess whether the outcomes are as expected.

In the case of trauma-sensitive schools, outcomes are measured indirect-ly through changes in student performance. Indicators are identified based on their known relationship to early trauma histories. With the exception of changes in social competence, most of the data can be mined from existing sources: school participation (improved attendance, reduction in the number of times tardy), behavior (decrease in number of office referrals, suspensions, and referrals to special education or Tier 3 interventions), and achievement (improved standardized test scores and measures of classroom performance) (Cole et al., 2013).

Social competence is defined as the "broad set of skills necessary to get along with others and behave constructively in groups" (Child Trends, 2015). Although peer rating systems or nominations are often used to measure social competence, Child Trends (2015) recommends the use of a quarterly teacher survey that measures changes in students' ability to take another's perspective, work well with peers, resolve problems without becoming aggressive, and behave in a manner appropriate to the situation. Given the close association between social competence and academic success, these easily collected data can be invaluable in monitoring student progress as a function of increased trauma-sensitive practice.

## IMPLICATIONS FOR EDUCATIONAL REFORM

Adopting a trauma-sensitive approach involves systemic changes that require close collaboration among all members of the school community. Unlike other reform measures that are implemented in a "top-down" manner, the paradigm shift required for a commitment to trauma-sensitive practices is so deep-seated that it requires a team approach to be successful.

The philosophy of trauma-sensitive schools challenges significant tenets of some educational practices, while offering strong support for others. The challenges lie primarily in the areas of behavior management and discipline where implementation moves beyond behaviorism to include a better understanding of adolescents' emotional development. Strong support is given to instructional best practices, such as differentiated instruction and dialogic teaching. These practices enable teachers to work with the brain's neuroplasticity to help students develop the resilience they need to overcome a traumatic past.

---

### WHAT ADMINISTRATORS CAN DO

1. Use the ACE questionnaire (see Appendix B) to guide the record review of students referred for alternative placements or special services. If they have three or more ACEs, include a discussion of trauma's impact on learning in planning interventions.

2. Review the number of referrals to alternative placement. Make sure that each referral includes documentation of the tiered interventions tried at each level and the effect of each intervention on student performance. If this information is not

included, request to see it before moving forward with the referral.

3. Provide teachers with professional development on de-escalating student behavior. Participate in the training with them so that they know you are available to back them up.

4. Provide teachers whose behaviors may trigger trauma reactions with one-on-one coaching about how reenactment works and how they can use a more trauma-sensitive approach going forward.

5. Work with district-level administrators to develop a comprehensive professional development plan to raise awareness of the need for trauma-sensitive schools.

6. Work with district-level administrators to recruit and hire consultants capable of providing districtwide professional development on trauma awareness and trauma-sensitive schools.

7. Facilitate the process of integrating trauma-sensitive benchmarks into overall school improvement plans.

8. Work with teachers to develop and implement an evaluation plan that includes process monitoring and student outcome goals. Schedule times for both types of data to be collected and reviewed.

9. Display the vision statement of trauma-sensitive schools throughout the building. Use time at faculty meetings to highlight a section of the vision statement and brainstorm ideas about what that element looks and sounds like on a daily basis. Monitor implementation of teachers' schedules to ensure that their time for co-planning and participation at tiered intervention meetings isn't being lost to school emergencies or repeated interruptions.

10. Acknowledge teachers' contribution to the implementation of a trauma-sensitive approach by sending letters to central office administrators who oversee their performance.

11. Build staff members' confidence in their ability to implement trauma-sensitive strategies by giving them specific feedback on observations you have made about how well they handled a potentially challenging situation.

### What Teachers Can Do

1. Commit to increasing the use of evidence-based practices in designing instruction and analyzing student behavior.

2. Commit to learning how to recognize "trauma flare-ups."

3. Commit to integrating opportunities to practice self-reflection and self-monitoring into everyday activities and routines.

4. Help students identify self-soothing behaviors they can use in the classroom to relieve stress and feel better.

5. Come prepared to actively participate in co-planning and tiered assistance team meetings. Use part of co-planning time to develop strategies for embedding a trauma-sensitive approach into classroom activities and routines.

6. Provide feedback to administrators about how to best utilize mental health agency support.

7. Work with peers to create a school culture that normalizes the effects of working with traumatized students. This gives teachers the support they need to address those effects in their own lives and work (Rosenbloom, Pratt, & Pearlman, 1995).

8. Use the "Components of a Trauma-Sensitive School" form (see Figure 9.1) to identify any components of the model that are currently being implemented at your school.

9. Be an active participant in the action planning process in your school. Work with others to reach consensus on priorities and tasks/timelines.

10. Reflect on the role release or role expansion issues that will need to be addressed to successfully transition to a trauma-sensitive school.

11. Volunteer to be part of a transition monitoring team or to work with colleagues to identify a measure of children's social competence to pilot at your school.

## CONCLUSION

The goal of the trauma-sensitive movement is to firmly establish trauma sensitivity within school cultures and practices. Its success relies on the ability of administrators to articulate a clear vision of a trauma-sensitive school and to put structures in place that allow the necessary collaboration and support. The more teachers perceive themselves as partners in the required change process, the more likely they are to support its full implementation. Careful planning and progress monitoring help integrate trauma-sensitive principles into broader frameworks of school reform that are committed to improved academic and social mastery. Continued advocacy for the rights of disenfranchised adolescents and recognition of the risks they face if their educational needs are left unattended or ignored emerge as fundamental issues to be addressed in any discussion of educational equity.

# Resources for
# Professional Development

*The ACE Study & Unaddressed Childhood Trauma (PPT): www.theannainstitute. org/presentations.html*

> Ann Jennings, PhD, of the Anna Institute in Rockland, Maine, developed this overview of ACE study outcomes and health-care costs.

*ACEs and Developmental Disabilities (PDF)*

> Dr. Steve Marcal, senior director of Behavioral Health Services from the Center for Disability Services in Albany, New York, created this PDF to increase the awareness of childhood adversity among professionals working with developmentally disabled children. The document can be used to train staff to be on the lookout for signs of trauma and respond in an appropriate manner.

*Adverse Childhood Experiences & Evidence-Based Home Visiting: http://www.nwcphp.org/ training/opportunities/webinars/adverse-childhood-experiences-and-evidence-based-home-visiting*

> This webinar (dated June 16, 2011) from the Northwest Center for Public Health Practice at the University of Washington features Kathy Carson from the Office of Public Health, Seattle and King County, and Laura Porter, Washington State Family Policy Council. According to the website, "New scientific discoveries about the lifelong impacts of adverse childhood experiences shed light on the intergenerational benefits of home visiting. Laura will share information about the ACE Study, including data from Washington State. Kathy will discuss some of the evidence of outcomes for home visiting and how understanding the impacts of childhood trauma can impact home visiting practice. This presentation is aimed at people working with young children and families and anyone interested in parenting and child development."

*Adverse Childhood Experiences and Their Relationship to Adult Well-Being and Disease: www.thenationalcouncil.org/wp-content/uploads/2012/11/Natl-Council-Webinar-8-2012.pdf*

> This presentation from the National Council for Behavioral Health provides an overview of the relationship between ACEs and detrimental health outcomes in adults. The presentation makes a strong case for medical

professionals to include questions about childhood experiences when treating conditions such as addiction, obesity, heart disease, and COPD.

*Ask the Experts: Trauma and Stress or Related Disorders in the DSM-5 (42 minutes): www.istss.org/education-research/online-learning/recordings.aspx?pid=WEB0813*

International Society of Traumatic Stress Studies (ISTSS) experts present this webinar, which focuses on the implications of the *Diagnostic and Statistical Manual of Mental Disorders, Fifth Edition* (DSM-5) criteria for assessment within the context of treatment—with an emphasis on the changes as well as new items and criteria—and how they might affect treatment or assessment before or after treatment. Panelists also discuss the recognition of a dissociative subtype of posttraumatic stress disorder (PTSD) within the DSM-5.

*Childhood Adversity Narratives (PowerPoint and PDF): www.canarratives.org*

Physicians and ACEs experts from University of North Carolina, Duke, University of California at San Francisco, and the New School developed a 50-slide PowerPoint presentation and PDF that the health-care community can use to educate policymakers and the public about ACEs. It might be a bit too complicated for the general public, but it's valuable for people in health care who want to educate the health-care community.

*Children's Mental Health Problems and the Need for Social Inclusion: http://www.slideserve.com/hollye/childrens-mental-health-problems-and-the-need-for-social-inclusion*

This PPT, created by SAMHSA, the Substance Abuse and Mental Health Services Administration, presents an overview of the issues that arise in helping children and families overcome the social isolation frequently experienced by children with mental illness. It is useful for agencies working with children and youth. It provides a comfortable framework for discussing the challenges involved and finding ways to overcome them.

*Creating a Trauma-Informed Team (Keynote: Ann Jennings, PhD; 93 minutes) (via acesconnection.com/blog/presentations)*

This webinar (2009) introduces the concepts of simple and complex trauma and discusses research related to re-traumatization within institutional and community settings. It is presented by the Division of Mental Health and Substance Abuse Services, Bureau of Prevention Treatment and Recovery.

*Dr. Robert Macy—Communities & Trauma Informed Care (2 minutes) (via acesconnection.com/blog/presentations)*

It is important for professionals who encounter trauma victims (in education, business, health care, the courts, social agencies, government, and more) to understand how to recognize, diagnose, and treat people who have suffered intense psychological and physical trauma as children—incidents called adverse childhood experiences (ACEs). Dr. Robert Macy talks about why a community effort is important.

*Dr. Bruce Perry interview on Blog Talk Radio about parents who adopt children with early trauma histories (1 hour): www.blogtalkradio.com/creatingafamily/2014/05/14/ parenting-abused-and-neglected-children*

> The purpose of this interview is to describe common behaviors observed among children with early trauma histories. It clarifies the difference among the threat-driven behaviors of traumatized children. It also offers parents strategies they can use to increase children's sense of safety and help them heal.

*The Impact of Trauma and Neglect on Young Children (1 hour): http://www.ctacny. org/training/impact-trauma-and-neglect-young-children*

> Dr. Bruce Perry presents this webinar from the New York Clinical Technical Assistance Center.

*Interpersonal Neurobiology (24 minutes) https://www.youtube.com/watch?v=LiyaSr5aeho*

> In this 2009 TEDx Blue Talk, Dr. Daniel Siegel explores the neural mechanisms beneath social and emotional intelligence and explores how they can be cultivated through reflective practices.

*National ACEs Summit: www.instituteforsafefamilies.org/national-summit-presentations*

> The 2013 National Summit on the Adverse Childhood Experiences Study findings and their impact on health and well-being was sponsored by the Institute for Safe Families and the Robert Wood Johnson Foundation. Videos and PDF files of many of the summit's presentations are available at the Institute for Safe Families website.

*Reclaiming Futures: Communities Helping Teens Overcome Drugs, Alcohol, & Crime: empty-memories.n6/science/felitti.pdf*

> New webinars are hosted almost every month by invited experts, and archived webinars are available on topics such as juvenile justice reform, juvenile drug courts, adolescent substance abuse treatment, and positive youth development.

*The Relationship of Adverse Childhood Experiences to Adult Health Status: https:// www.ncbi.nlm.nih.gov/pubmed/12407494*

> This is Dr. Felitti's original discussion of the effects of adverse childhood experiences on adult health status. It is a classic in the field that marks a turning point in the field's understanding of the relationship between childhood experiences and adult mental and physical well-being.

*Strong Communities Raise Strong Kids (PowerPoint): www.pent.ca.gov/mt/aces.pptx*

> Arizona Regional Child Abuse Prevention Councils (2011) put this PowerPoint together and has been showing it to dozens of communities

across the state. It reviews ACE study, brain research, cost consequences of not preventing ACEs, and how families and communities can build resilience factors to prevent ACEs.

*THRIVE's Trauma-Informed Webinar Trainings: www.thriveinitiative.org/webinars*

THRIVE webinars embody system of care principles and are well suited for agency orientations and group or individual viewing. Registration for each webinar is required, and will give access to the *Guide to Trauma-Informed Organizational Development* and other resources. THRIVE is Maine's graduated System of Care, and receives funding from Maine's Department of Corrections Division of Juvenile Services and the federal Substance Abuse and Mental Health Services Administration.

*Trauma: A Public Health Crisis in Western New York Conference: socialwork.buffalo. edu/resources/conferences-special-events/trauma/conference.html*

This webinar features Dr. Sandra Bloom and Dr. Robert Anda, who on March 12 and 13, 2010, spoke at the Trauma: A Public Health Crisis in Western New York conference, sponsored by the Community Health Foundation of Western and Central New York. Conference participants learned to recognize the role of trauma in the lives of children, to identify the effects of adverse childhood experiences on adult health risk behaviors and diseases, and to apply the tenets of the sanctuary model to provide trauma-informed treatment and care. Furthermore, this conference enabled participants to collaborate with one another to form a network of community leaders and activists.

*Trauma-Informed Care for Women Experiencing Homelessness and Their Children (1 hour): www.usich.gov/tools-for-action/webinar-trauma-informed-care*

This webinar, sponsored by the U.S. Interagency Council on Homelessness, explores the ways homeless services programs can use a trauma-informed care model to better serve mothers and their children and help break through the cycle of trauma and homelessness. The goal of the webinar (dated May 9, 2012) is to share information on how to improve the trauma confidence of your organization.

*Trauma-Informed Practice with Children and Youth in the Child Welfare System (65 minutes): www.nrcpfc.org/webcasts/28.html*

This webcast features Erika Tullberg, an assistant professor of research at the New York University Child Study Center and director of the Atlas Project, an Administration for Children and Families–funded effort to address trauma and other mental health issues in New York State's child welfare system, and Dr. Glenn N. Saxe (the Arnold Simon Professor and Chair, Department of Child and Adolescent Psychiatry, New York University Child Study Center), a physician-scientist with a focus on the psychiatric consequences of traumatic events in children. The focus of the webinar is foster care and birth parents. Other resources are also included on this website. The webinar (dated February 6, 2013) is sponsored by the National Resource Center for Permanency and Family Connections.

*Treating Trauma in Kids: http://www.cehd.umn.edu/fsos/projects/ambit/pdf/Wilson%20Presentation.pdf*

Charles Wilson, executive director of the Chadwick Center for Children and Families at Rady Children's Hospital–San Diego, describes his work developing a trauma-informed systems approach that treats children within the child welfare system. This presentation (dated May 27, 2010) is applicable to the field of juvenile justice as well.

*Violence Prevention–Dr. Sandra Bloom (3 minutes): vimeo.com/18028256*

In 2010, Dr. Sandra Bloom talked to the Congreso Internacional JUCO-NI in Mexico about preventing violence via community/family health. (The video is presented in English.)

APPENDIX B

# Finding Your ACE Score

While you were growing up, during your first 18 years of life:

1.  Did a parent or other adult in the household often or very often swear
    at you, insult you, put you down, or humiliate you? Or act in a way that
    made you afraid that you might be physically hurt?

    Yes   No

2.  Did a parent or other adult in the household often or very often push,
    grab, slap, or throw something at you? Or ever hit you so hard that you
    had marks or were injured?

    Yes   No

3.  Did an adult or person at least 5 years older than you ever touch or
    fondle you or have you touch their body in a sexual way? Or attempt or
    actually have oral, anal, or vaginal intercourse with you?

    Yes   No

4.  Did you often or very often feel that no one in your family loved you or
    thought you were important or special? Or your family didn't look out
    for one another, feel close to one another, or support one another?

    Yes   No

5.  Did you often or very often feel that you didn't have enough to eat, had
    to wear dirty clothes, and had no one to protect you? Or your parents
    were too drunk or too high to take care of you, or take you to the doctor
    if you needed it?

    Yes   No

6.  Were your parents ever separated or divorced?

    Yes   No

7.  Was you mother or stepmother:

    *   Often or very often pushed, grabbed, slapped, or had something
        thrown at her?

- Or sometimes, often, or very often kicked, bitten, hit with a fist, or hit with something hard? Or ever repeatedly hit at least a few minutes or threatened with a gun or knife?

Yes   No

8.  Did you ever live with someone who was a problem drinker or alcoholic or who used street drugs?

    Yes   No

9.  Was a household member depressed or mentally ill, or did a household member attempt suicide?

    Yes   No

10. Did a household member go to prison?

    Yes   No


Now add up your Yes answers: This is your ACE score.

(Retrieved from www.acestudy.org/yahoo_site_admin/assets/docs/ACE_Cal-culator-English.127193712.pdf)

# References

ABA Juvenile Justice Committee. (2001). *Zero tolerance policy report.* Washington, DC: Author.

Abenavoli, R. M., Jennings, P. A., Greenberg, M. T., Harris, A. R., & Katz, D. A. (2013). The protective effects of mindfulness against burnout among educators. *Psychology of Education Review, 37* (2), 57–69.

Abraham-Cook, S. (2012). The prevalence and correlates of compassion fatigue, compassion satisfaction, and burnout among teachers working in high-poverty urban public schools (Doctoral dissertation, Seton Hall University). Retrieved from http://scholarship.shu.edu/cgi/viewcontent.cgi?article=2820&context=dissertations

Abrutyn, S., & Mueller, A. S. (2014). Are suicidal behaviors contagious in adolescence? Using longitudinal data to examine suicide suggestion. *American Sociological Review, 79*(2): 211–227. doi: 10.1177/0003122413519445

Ahmed, S. P., Bittencourt-Hewitt, A., & Sebastian, C. L. (2015). Neurocognitive bases of emotion regulation development in adolescence. *Developmental Cognitive Neuroscience, 15*, 11–25.

Ainsworth, M. D. (1964). Patterns of attachment behavior shown by the infant in interaction with his mother. *Merrill-Palmer Quarterly of Behavior and Development, 10*, 51–58.

Anda, R. F., Felitti, V. J., Bremner, J. D., Walker, J. D., Whitfield, C., Perry, B. D., & Giles, W. H. (2006). The enduring effects of abuse and related adverse experiences in childhood: A convergence of evidence from neurobiology and epidemiology. *European Archives of Psychiatry and Clinical Neuroscience, 256*(3), 174–186.

Anderson, J. (2016). The teen-age brain under construction. *The college speaks: American College of Pediatricians.* Retrieved from https://www.acpeds.org/the-college-speaks/position-statements/parenting-issues/the-teenage-brain-under-construction

Anderson, L.W. & Krathwohl, D. R. (2001). *A taxonomy for learning, teaching, and assessing: A revision of Bloom's taxonomy of educational objectives.* New York, NY: Longman.

Arbona, C., Olvers, N., Rodriguez, N., Hagan, J., Linares, A., & Wiesner. M. (2010). Acculturative stress among documented and undocumented Latino immigrants in the United States. *Hispanic Journal of Behavioral Science, 32*(3), 362–384.

Asam, K. (2015). *Trauma-sensitive schools.* Trauma webinar: University of Vermont. [Webinar]. Retrieved from http://www.uvm.edu/~cdci/best/pbswebsite/TRAUMA.html

Balfanz, R., & Byrnes, V. (2012). *The importance of being in school: A report on absenteeism in the nation's public schools.* Baltimore, MD: Johns Hopkins University Center for Social Organization of Schools.

Balfour, D., & Neff, P. (1993). Predicting and managing turnover in human service agencies: A case study of an organization in crisis. *Public Personnel Management, 22,* 473–486.

Bandura, A. (1982). Self-efficacy mechanism in human agency. *American Psychologist, 37,* 122–147.

Belsky, J. & de Hann, M. (2011). Annual research review: Parenting and children's brain development: The end of the beginning. *Journal of Child Psychology and Psychiatry, and Allied Disciplines, 52*(4), 409–428.

Benson, P. L., & Scales, P. C. (2009). The definition and preliminary measurement of thriving in adolescence. *Journal of Positive Psychology, 4*(1), 85–104.

Bergin, C., & Bergin, D. (2009). Attachment in the classroom. *Educational Psychology Review, 21,* 141–170.

Blad, E., & Harwin, A. (2017). Black students more likely to be arrested at school. *Education Week,* May 30, 2017. Bethesda, MD: Editorial Projects in Education, Inc.

Bloom, S. L., & Farragher, B. (2011). *Destroying sanctuary: The crisis in human service delivery systems.* New York, NY: Oxford University Press.

Bloom, S. L., & Farragher, B. (2013). *Restoring sanctuary: A new operating system for trauma-informed systems of care.* New York, NY: Oxford University Press.

Blum, R. W. (2005). A case for school connectedness. *Educational Leadership, 62*(7), 16–20.

Borman, G. D., & Dowling, N. M. (2008, September). Teacher attrition and retention: A meta-analytic and narrative review of the research. *Review of Educational Research, 78,* 367–409.

Boykin, W., & Noguera, P. (2011). *Creating the opportunity to learn: Moving from research to practice to close the achievement gap.* Alexandria, VA: Association for Supervision and Curriculum Development.

Brent, D., Perper, J., Goldstein, C., Kolko, D., Allan, M., Allman, C., & Zelnak, J. (1988). Risk factors for adolescent suicide: A comparison of adolescent suicide victims with suicidal inpatients. *Archives of General Psychiatry, 45,* 581–588.

Breslau, N., Wilcox, H. C., Storr, C. L., Lucia, V. C., & Anthony, J. C. (2004). Trauma exposure and posttraumatic stress disorder: A study of youths in urban America. *Journal of Urban Health: Bulletin of the New York Academy of Medicine, 81,* 530–544.

Bretherton, I., & Munholland, K. A. (1999). Internal working models revisited. In J. Cassidy & P. R. Shaver (Eds.), *Handbook of attachment: Theory, research, and clinical applications* (pp. 89–111). New York, NY: Guilford Press.

Briere, J., & Lanktree, C. B. (2012). *Treating complex trauma in adolescents and young adults.* Thousand Oaks, CA: Sage Publications, Inc.

Briere, J., & Spinazzola, J. (2005). Phenomenology and psychological assessment of complex posttraumatic stress. *Journal of Traumatic Stress, 18*(5), 401–412.

Bronfenbrenner, U. (2005). *Making human beings human: Bioecological perspectives on human development.* Thousand Oaks, CA: Sage Publications.

Brown, A & Finkelhor, D. (1986). Impact of child sexual abuse. *Psychological Bulletin, (99), 1,* 66-77.

Brown, S. A., Tapert, S. F., Granholm, E., & Delis, D. C. (2000). Neurocognitive functioning of adolescents: Effects of protracted alcohol use. *Alcoholism: Clinical and Experimental Research, 24*(2), 164–171.

Bruner, J. (1996). *The culture of education.* Cambridge, MA: Harvard University Press.

Bryk, A. S., Sebring, P. B., Allensworth, E., Luppescu, S., & Easton, J. Q. (2010). *Organizing schools for improvement: Lessons from Chicago.* Chicago, IL: University of Chicago Press.

Caine, R., & Caine, G. (1990). Understanding a brain-based approach to learning and teaching. *Educational Leadership,* 66–70.

Callianeo, A., Macchi, F., Piazzotta, G., Veronice, B., Bocchio-Chiavetto, L., Riva, M. A., & Pariante, C. M. (2015). Inflammation and neuronal plasticity: A link between childhood trauma and depression pathogenesis. *Frontiers of Cellular Neuroscience, 48*(2), 66–70.

Carter, R. T. (2007). Racism and psychological and emotional injury: Recognizing and assessing race-based traumatic stress. *The Counseling Psychologist, 35*(1), 13–105.

Casey, B. J., Jones, R. H., & Hare, T. A. (2008). The adolescent brain. *Annals of the New York Academy of Science, 1124,* 111–126.

Cassidy, J. (2001). Intimacy: An attachment perspective. *Attachment and Human Development, 3*(2), 121–155.

CAST (2011). Universal Design for Learning Guidelines version 2.0. Retrieved from http://www.udlcenter.org/aboutudl/udlguidelines

Catalano, S. A. (2006). *Criminal victimization, 2006.* Washington, DC: Bureau of Justice Statistics. Retrieved from http://www.ojp.usdoj. gov/bjs/pub/pdf/cv06.pdf

Center for Youth Wellness. (2014). *An unhealthy dose of stress* [White paper]. Retrieved from http://bit.ly/ACEswhitepaper

Cerrone, K. M. (1999). The gun free school act, 1994: Zero tolerance takes aim at procedural due process. *Pace Law Review, 20*(1), 131–188.

Chalk, R., & Phillips, D. (Eds.). (1996). *Youth development and neighborhood influences: Summary of a workshop.* Washington, DC: National Academies Press.

Chang, M. L. (2009). An appraisal perspective of teacher burnout: examining the emotional work of teachers. *Educational Psychology Review, 21,* 193–218.

Child Trends. (2015). *Social competence #14.* Retrieved from https://www.childtrends. org/research/research-by-topic/positive-indicators-project/social-competence/

Cicchetti, D. (2006). Development and psychopathology. In D. Ciccetti & D. J. Cohen (Eds.), *Developmental psychopathology: Theory and method* (2nd ed., pp. 1–23), New York, NY: Wiley.

Claassen, R., & Claassen, R. (2008). *Discipline that restores: Strategies to create respect, co-operation, and responsibility in the classroom.* Charleston, SC: BookSurge Publishing.

Cloitre, M., Stolbach, B. C., Herman, J. L., van der Kolk, B., Pynoos, R., Wang, J., & Petkova, E. (2009, October). A developmental approach to complex PTSD: Childhood and adult cumulative trauma as predictors of system complexity. *Journal of Traumatic Stress, 22,* 399–408.

Cole, S. F., Eisner, A., Gregory, M., & Ristuccia, J. (2013). *Creating and advocating for trauma-sensitive schools.* Boston, MA: Massachusetts Advocates for Children and Harvard Law School.

Cole, S. F., O'Brien, J. G., Gadd, M. G., Ristuccia, J., Wallace, D. L., & Gregory, M. (2005). *Helping traumatized children learn: Supportive school environments for children traumatized by family violence.* Boston, MA: Massachusetts Advocates for Children.

Collaborative for Academic, Social, and Emotional Learning (CASEL). (2004). *Creating connections for student success: The CASEL 2003 annual report.* Retrieved from http:// static1.squarespace.com/static/513f79f9e4b05ce7b70e9673/t/526a22f3e4b 0f35a9effc404/1382687475283/creating-connections-for-student-success.pdf

Corcoran, K., & Roberts, A. R. (Eds.). (2015). *Social workers' desk reference.* New York, NY: Oxford University Press.

Cozolino, L. (2006). *The neuroscience of human relationships: Attachment and the developing social brain.* New York, NY: W. W. Norton.

Craig, S. E. (2008). *Reaching and teaching children who hurt: Strategies for your classroom.* Baltimore, MD: Brookes Publishing Co.

Crews, F. T., Braun, C. J, Hoplight, B., Switzer, R. C., III, & Knapp, D. J. (2000). Binge ethanol consumption causes differential brain damage in young adolescent rats compared with adult rats. *Alcoholism: Clinical and Experimental Research, 24,* 1712–1723.

Crittenden, P. M. (1998). Dangerous behaviors and dangerous contexts: A 35-year perspective on research on the developmental effects of child physical abuse. In P. K. Trickett & C. J. Schellenbach (Eds.), *Violence against children in the family and the community* (pp. 11–38). Washington, DC: American Psychological Association.

Cullen, M. (2012, January 12). Stopping teacher burn-out. *Greater Good Magazine.*

De Bellis, M. D., Clark, D. B., Beers, S. R., et al. (2000). Hippocampal volume in adolescent-onset alcohol use disorders. *American Journal of Psychiatry, 157,* 737–744.

Diamond, A. (2013). Executive functions. *Annual Review of Psychology, 64,* 135–168. doi: 10.1146/annurev-psych-113011-143750.

Dorado, J. (2008) Healthy environments and response to trauma in schools. San Francisco, CA: University of California, San Francisco.

Elais, M. (2013). The school-to-prison pipeline. *Teaching Tolerance, 43,* 39–40.

Emdin, C. (2016). *For white folks who teach in the hood . . . and the rest of y'all too: Reality pedagogy and urban education.* Boston, MA: Beacon Press.

Epstein, R. (2015). *The sexual abuse to prison pipeline: The girls' story.* Washington, DC: Georgetown Law Center on Poverty and Inequality.

Epstein, R. (2016, June 1). Policing girls of color. *Education Week.* Retrieved from www. edweek.org/ew/articles/2016/06/01/policing-girls-of-color-in-schools.html

Farragher, B., & Yanosy, S. (2005). Creating a trauma-sensitive culture in residential treatment. *Therapeutic Communities: The International Journal for Therapeutic and Supportive Organizations, 26,* 96–113.

Felitti, V. J., Anda, R. F., Nordenberg, D., Williamson, D. F., Spitz, A. M., Edwards, V., . . . Marks, J. S. (1998, May). Relationship of childhood abuse and household dysfunction to many of the leading causes of death in adults: The adverse childhood experiences (ACE) study. *American Journal of Preventive Medicine, 14,* 245–258.

Figley, C. R. (Ed.) (2002). *Treating compassion fatigue.* New York, NY: Brunner-Mazel.

Finkelhor, D., & Dzuiba-Leatherman, J. (1994). Victimization of children. *American Psychologist, 49*(3), 173–183.

Finkelhor, D., & Ormrod, R. (2000). *Juvenile victims of property crimes.* Washington, DC: Juvenile Justice Bulletin.

Finkelhor, D., Ormrod, R. K., & Turner, H. A. (2007). Poly-victimization: A neglected component in child victimization. *Child Abuse and Neglect, 31,* 7–26.

Finkelhor, D., Ormrod, R. K., Turner, H. A., & Hamby, S. L. (2005). The victimization of children and youth: A comprehensive national survey. *Child Maltreatment, 10*(1), 5–25.

Finkelhor, D., Ormrod, R. K., Turner, H. A., & Hamby, S. (2010). Trends in childhood violence and abuse exposure: Evidence from two national surveys. *Archives of Pediatrics & Adolescent Medicine, 164*(3), 238–242.

Finkelhor, D., Turner, H., Hamby, S., & Ormrod, R. K. (2011). *Poly-victimization: Children's exposure to multiple types of violence, crime, and abuse.* Washington, DC: Office of Juvenile Justice and Delinquency Prevention.

Finkelhor, D., Turner, H., Ormrod, R. K., & Hamby, S. (2011). Poly-victimization in a developmental context. *Journal of Child and Adolescent Trauma, 4,* 291–300.

Flannery, M. E. (2015). The school-to-prison pipeline: Time to shut it down. Retrieved from neatoday.org/2015/01/05/school-prison-pipeline-time-shut

Ford, J. D., Chapman, J., Mack, M., & Pearson, G. (2006). Pathways from traumatic child victimization to delinquency: Implications for juvenile and permanency court proceedings and decisions. *Juvenile & Family Court Journal, 57*(1), 13–26.

Ford, J. D., & Russo, E. (2006). Trauma-focused present-centered emotional self-regulation approach to integrated treatment for posttraumatic stress and addiction: Trauma adaptive recovery group education and therapy (TARGET). *American Journal of Psychotherapy, 60,* 335–355.

Fosha, D. (2003). Dyadic regulation and experiential work with emotions and relatedness in trauma and disorganized attachment. In M.F. Solomon & D.J. Siegel (Eds.), *Healing trauma: attachment, mind, body, and brain* (pp. 221–281). New York, NY: W. W. Norton.

Frost, R. (1969). *The poetry of Robert Frost: The collected poems, complete and unabridged.* New York, NY: Henry Holt.

Fuhrmann, D., Knoll, L. J., & Blakemore, S. J. (2015). Adolescence as a sensitive period of brain development. *Trends in Cognitive Science, 19*(10), 558–566.

Garbarino, J., Kostelny, K., & Dubrow, N. (1991). What children can tell us about living in danger. *American Psychologist, 46*(4), 376–383.

Gentile, A., De Vito, F., Fresegna, D., Musella, A., Buttari, S., Mandolesi, G., & Centonze, D. (2015). Exploring the role of microglia in mood disorders associated with experimental multiple sclerosis. *Frontiers in Cellular Neuroscience, 9,* 243.

Gerson, R., & Rappaport, N. (2013). Traumatic stress and post-traumatic stress disorder in youth: Recent research findings on clinical impact, assessment, and treatment. *Journal of Adolescent Health, 52,* 137–143.

Giacobbe, G. A., Traynelis-Yurek, E., Powell, L. M., & Laursen, E. (Eds.). (1994). *Positive peer culture: A selected bibliography on positive peer culture.* Richmond, VA: G & T Publishing.

Giancola, P. R., Shoal, G. D., & Mezzich, A. C. (2001). Constructive thinking, executive functioning, antisocial behavior, and drug use involvement in adolescent females with a substance use disorder. *Experiments in Clinical Psychopharmacology, 9*, 215–227.

Gibbs, S., & Miller, A. (2014). Teachers' resilience and well-being: a role for educational psychology. *Teachers and Teaching: Theory and Practice, 20*, 609–621. doi:10.1 080/13540602.2013.844408

Giedd, J. N. (2004). Structural magnetic resonance imaging of the adolescent brain. *Annals of the New York Academy of Science, 1021*(1), 77–85.

Giedd, J. N. (2015). Adolescent neuroscience of addiction: A new era. *Developmental Cognitive Neuroscience, 16*, 192–193.

GLSEN. (2015). 2015 National school climate survey: LGBTQ students experience pervasive harassment and discrimination, but school-based supports can make a difference. Retrieved from http://www.glsen.org/article/2015-national-school-climate-survey

Goff, P. A., Jackson, M. C., DiLeone, B. A., Culotta, C. M., & DiTomasso, N. A. (2014). The essence of innocence: Consequences of dehumanizing Black children. *Journal of Personality and Psychology, 106*(4), 526–545. doi: 10.1037/a0035663

Grant, B. F., & Dawson, D. A. (1997). Age at onset of alcohol use and its associations with DSM-IV alcohol abuse and dependence: Results from the National Longitudinal Alcohol Epidemiologic Survey. *Journal of Substance Abuse, 10*(2), 163–173.

Green, E. (2014). *Building a better teacher: How teaching works (and how to teach it to everyone).* New York, NY: Norton.

Greenspan, S. I. (1997). *The growth of the mind and the endangered nature of intelligence.* Reading, MA: Perseus.

Griffin, K. (2015). 4 ways teachers can address micro aggressions in the classroom. Retrieved from https://www.noodle.com/articles/microaggressions-in-the-classroom-the-teachers-role

Guerri, C. &, Pascual, M. (2010). Mechanisms involved in the neurotoxic, cognitive, and neurobehavioral effects of alcohol consumption during adolescence. *Alcohol, 44*, 15–23.

Guin, K. (2004, August). Chronic teacher turnover in urban elementary schools. *Educational Policy Analysis Archives, 12*(42). Retrieved from http://epaa.asu.edu/epaa/v12n42.pdf

Haley, C., & Hughes, J. L. (2010). Adolescent suicide attempters: Latest research & promising interventions. Texas Suicide Prevention Symposium, June 10, 2010. Retrieved from texassuicideprevention.org./wp-content/uploads/2013/06/AdolescentSuicideAttempters

Hamby, S., Finkelhor, D., Turner, H., & Kracke, K. (2011). *The juvenile victimization questionnaire toolkit.* Retrieved from http://www.unh.edu/ccrc/jvq/index_new.html

Hammond, Z. (2015). *Culturally responsive teaching and the brain: Promoting authentic engagement and rigor among culturally and linguistically diverse students.* Thousand Oaks, CA: Corwin.

Hann, N. (1992). The assessment of coping, defense, and stress. In L. Goldberger & S. Breznitz (Eds.), *Handbook of stress: Theoretical and clinical aspects* (2nd ed., pp. 258–273). Toronto, Canada: The Free Press.

Hargreaves, A. (2000). Mixed emotions: Teachers' perceptions of their interactions with students. *Teaching and Teacher Education, 16,* 811–826. doi:10.1016/S0742-051X(00)00028-7

Haslam, N., Rothschild, L., & Ernst, D. (2000). Essentialist beliefs about social categories. *British Journal of Social Psychology, 39,* 113–127.

Heilzeg, N. A. (2009). Education not incarceration: Interrupting the school to prison pipeline, *Forum on Public Policy, 2,* 1–21.

Hill, A. C. (2011). The cost of caring: An investigation of the effects of teaching traumatized children in urban, elementary settings (Doctoral dissertation, University of Massachusetts). Retrieved from http://scholarworks.umass.edu/cgi/viewcontent.cgi?article=1396&context=open_access_dissertations

Hingson, R. W., & Kenkel, D. (2004). Social, health, and economic consequences of underage drinking. In National Research Council and Institute of Medicine, *Reducing underage drinking: A collective responsibility.* Washington, DC: The National Academies Press.

Hughes, C. M., McElnay, J. C., & Fleming, G. T. (2001). Benefits and risks of self-medication. *Drug Safety, 24*(14), 1027–1037. doi: 10.2165/00002018-20011241-00002

Hughes, D. A., & Baylin, J. (2012). *Brain-based parenting: The neuroscience of caregiving for healthy attachment.* New York, NY: Norton.

Human Rights Campaign (2013). *Growing up LGBT in America: HRC youth survey report key findings.* Washington, DC: Author.

Ingersoll, R. M., & Smith, T. M. (2003). The wrong solution to the teacher shortage. *Educational Leadership, 60*(8), 30–33.

Jablow, P. (2014). Addressing childhood trauma in schools. *The Philadelphia Public School Notebook: Focus on Behavioral Health in Schools, 22*(3). Retrieved from http://thenotebook.org/december-2014/147967/addressing-childhood-trauma-schools-expert-views

Jagadeesan, L. M. (2012). Attachment and social behavior in middle childhood: A comparison of maltreated and non-maltreated children [Dissertation]. University of Minnisota. Retrieved from http://purl.umn.edu/137494

Jain, S., Buka, S. L., Subramanian, S. L., & Molnar, B. E. (2012). Protective factors for youth exposed to violence: Role of developmental assets in building emotional resilience. *Youth Violence and Juvenile Justice, 10*(1), 107–129.

Jennings, P. A., & Greenberg, M. T. (2009). The prosocial classroom: Teacher social and emotional competence in relation to student and classroom outcomes. *Review of Educational Research, 79,* 491–525. doi:10.3102/0034654308325693

Jennings, P., Snowberg, K., Coccia, M., & Greenberg, M. (2011). Improving classroom learning environments by cultivating awareness and resilience in education: Results of two pilot studies. *Journal of Classroom Instruction, 46*(1), 37–48.

Jensen, E. (2008). *Brain-based learning: The new paradigm of teaching.* Thousand Oaks, CA: Corwin Press.

Jensen, F. E., & Nutt, A. M. (2015). *The teenage brain*. New York, NY: Harper.

Johnson, D., & Johnson, D. (1990). *Cooperative learning: Warm ups, grouping strategies and group activities*. Edina, MN: Interaction Book Company.

Johnson, S., Cooper, C., Cartwright, S., Donald, I., Taylor, P. J., & Millet, C. (2005). The experience of work related stress across occupations. *Journal of Managerial Psychology, 20*(2), 178–187. doi:10.1108/02683940510579803

Johnson, S. B., Riley, A. W., Granger, D. A., & Riis, J. (2013). The science of early life toxic stress for pediatric practice and advocacy. *Pediatrics, 131*, 319–327. doi:10.1542/peds.2012-0469

Johnston, P. H. (2012). *Opening minds: Using language to change lives*. Portland, ME: Stenhouse.

Jones, R. T., Hadder, J. M., Carvajal, F., Chapman, S., & Alexander, A. (2006) *Conducting research in diverse, minority, and marginalized communities*. In F. Norris, S. Galea, M. J. Friedman, P.J. Watson (Eds.), *Methods for disaster mental health research* (pp. 265–277). New York, NY: Guilford Press.

Kagan, J. (2002). *Surprise, uncertainty, and mental structures*. Cambridge, MA: Harvard University Press.

Kauffman, J. M., & Badar, J. (2013). How we might make special education for students with emotional or behavioral disorders less stigmatizing. *Behavioral Disorders, 39*, 16–27.

Kessler, R. C., Berglund, P., Demler, D., Jin, R., Merikangas, K. R., & Waller, E. F. (2005). Lifetime prevalence and age of onset distributions of DSM-IV disorders in national comorbidity survey replication. *Archives of General Psychiatry, 2*(6), 593–602.

Kimmel, M. (2008). *Guyland: The perilous world where boys become men*. New York, NY: HarperCollins.

Kira, I. A. (2010). Etiology and treatment of post-cumulative traumatic stress disorders in different cultures. *Traumatology, 16*(4), 128–141. Retrieved from http://www.irre.org/sites/default/files/publication_pdfs/Klem_and_Connell_2004_JOSH_article.pdf

Klassen, R. M., Perry, N. E., & Frenzel, A. C. (2012). Teachers' relatedness with students: An underemphasized component of teachers' basic psychological needs. *Journal of Educational Psychology, 104*, 150–165. doi:10.1037/a0026253

Klem, A. M., & Connell, J. P. (2004). Relationships matter: Linking teacher support to student engagement and achievement. *Journal of School Health, 74*(7), 262–273.

Klusmann, U., Kunter, M., Trautwein, U., Ludtke, O., & Baumert, J. (2008, August). Teacher occupational well-being and quality of instruction: The important role of self-regulatory patterns. *Journal of Educational Psychology, 100*, 702–715. doi:10.1037/0022-0663.100.3.702

Kohli, R., & Solórzano, D. G. (2012). Teachers, please learn our names: Racial micro-aggressions and the K–12 classroom. *Race, Ethnicity and Education, 15*(4), 441–462.

Ladson-Billings, G. (1995). Toward a theory of culturally relevant pedagogy. *American Educational Research Journal, 32*(3), 465–491.

Lansford, J. E., Malone, P. S., Stevens, K. I., Dodge, K. A., Bates, J. E., & Pettit, G. S. (2006). Developmental trajectories of externalizing and internalizing behaviors: Factors underlying resilience in physically abused children. *Development and Psychopathology, 18,* 35–56. doi:10.1017/S0954579406060032

Larson, R. W. (2000). Toward a psychology of positive youth development. *American Psychologist, 55*(1), 170–183. doi: 1037//00003-066X.55.1.170

Latsch, D. C., Netl, J. C., & Humbelin, O. A. (2016). Poly-victimization and its relationship to emotional and social adjustment in adolescence: Evidence from a national survey in Switzerland. *Psychology of Violence, 7*(1): 1–11. doi 10.1037/a0039993.

Leahy, M. (2015). When experts miss trauma in children. *Psych Central.* Retrieved from https://psychcentral.com/lib/when-experts-miss-trauma-in-children/

Lemov, D. (2010). *Teach like a champion: 49 techniques that put students on the path to college (K–12).* San Francisco, CA: Jossey-Bass.

Lerner, R. M., Fisher, C. B., & Weinberg, R. A. (2000). Toward a science for and of the people: Promoting civil society through the application of developmental science. *Child Development, 71*(1), 11–30. doi: 10.1111/1467-8624.00113

Levine, M. D. (2002). *A mind at a time.* New York, NY: Simon & Schuster.

Levine, P., & Kline, M. (2006). *Trauma through a child's eyes: Awakening the ordinary miracle of healing.* Berkeley, CA: North Atlantic Books.

Linley, P. A., & Joseph, S. (2004) Positive change following trauma and adversity: A review. *Journal of Traumatic Stress, 17*(1), 11–21.

Lipschitz, D. S., Winegar, R. K., Nicolaou, A. L., Hartnick, E., Wolfson, M., & Southwick, S. M. (1999). Perceived abuse and neglect as risk factors for suicidal behavior in adolescent inpatients. *Journal of Nervous Mental Disorders. 187,* 32–39.

Loukas, A., Roalson, L., & Herrera, D. (2010). School connectedness buffers the effects of negative family relations and poor effortful control on early adolescent conduct problems. *Journal of Research on Adolescence, 20,* 13–22. doi: 10.1111/j.1532-7795.2009.00632.x

Luna, B., & Sweeney, J. A. (2004). The emergence of collaborative brain function: fMRI studies of the development of response inhibition. *Annals of the New York Academy of Sciences, 1021,* 296–309.

Luria, A. R. (1966). *Human brain and psychological processes.* New York, NY: Harper & Row.

Maiese, M. (2004). Retributive justice: Beyond intractability. In G. Burgess & H. Burgess (Eds.), *Conflict Information Consortium.* Boulder, CO: University of Colorado. Retrieved from http://www.beyondintractability.org/essay/retributive-justice

Main, M., & Solomon, J. (1990). Procedures for identifying disorganized/disoriented infants during the Ainsworth Strange Situation. In M. Greenberg, D. Cicchetti, & M. Cummings (Eds.), *Attachment in the preschool years* (pp. 121–160). Chicago, IL: University of Chicago Press.

Maple, M., Cerel, J., Sanford, R., Pearce,, T., & Jordan, J. (2016). Is exposure to suicide beyond kin associated with risk for suicidal behavior? A systemic review of the evidence. *Suicide and Life Threatening Behavior, 131*(1), 100–107. Washington, DC: American Association of Suicidology.

Martin, H. (1979). Child abuse and development. *Child Abuse and Neglect, 3,* 415–421.

Masten, A. S., & Coatsworth, J. D. (1995). Competence, resilience and psychopathology. In D. Cicchetti & D. Cohen (Eds.), *Developmental psychopathology: Risk, disorder and adaption* (Vol. 2, pp. 715–752). New York, NY: Wiley.

Maxwell, L. (2014), School enrollment hits a majority–minority milestone. *Education Week.* Retrieved from http://www.edweek.org/ew/articles/2014/08/20/01 demographics.h34.html

McCambridge, J., McAlaney, J., & Rowe, R. (2011). Adult consequences of late adolescent alcohol consumption: A systematic review of cohort studies. *PLOS Medicine, 8*(2): e1000413. doi: 10.1371/journal.pmed.1000413

McCarthy, M. M. (2013). Microglia: A piece of the puzzle of puberty. *Nature Neuroscience, 16,* 13–15. doi: 10.1523JNEUROSCI1268-12 2013

McCrory, E., De Brito, S., & Viding, E. (2011). The impact of childhood maltreatment: A review of neurological and genetic factors. *Frontiers in Psychiatry, 2*(48), 1–14. doi:10.3389/fpsyt.2011.00048

McElhaney, K. B., Allen, J. P., Stephenson, J. C., & Hare, A. L. (2009). Attachment and autonomy during adolescence. *Handbook of Adolescent Psychology, 1:II:11.* doi: 10.1002/9780470479193.adlpsy001012

McInerney, M., & McKlindon, A. (2014). *Unlocking the door to learning: Trauma-informed classrooms and transformational schools.* Philadelphia, PA: Educational Law Center.

McIntosh, J. L. (2000). Epidemiology of adolescent suicide in the United States. In R. Maris, S. S. Canetto, J. L. McIntosh, M. M. Silverman, M. Morton (Eds.), *Review of suicidology,* (pp. 3–33). New York, NY: Guilford Press.

Meltzoff, A. N. (2002). Imitation as a mechanism of social cognition: Origins of empathy, theory of mind and the representation of action. In N. U. Goswami (Ed.), *Blackwell handbook of childhood cognitive development* (pp. 6–25). Oxford, UK: Blackwell Publishers.

Mikulincer, M., & Shaver, P. R. (2007). *Attachment in adulthood: Structures, dynamics, and change.* New York, NY: Guilford Press.

Modecki, J., Minchin, K. L., Harbaugh, A. G., Guerra, N. G., & Runions, K. C. (2014). Bullying prevalence across contexts: A meta-analysis measuring cyberbullying and traditional bullying. *Journal of Adolescent Health, 55*(5), 602–611.

Money, J. (1982). Child abuse: Growth failure, I.Q. deficit, and learning disability. *Journal of Learning Disabilities, 120,* 439–446.

Mullinar, L., & Hunt, C. (Eds.) (1997). *Breaking the silence: Survivors of child abuse speak out.* Sydney, Australia: Hodder & Stoughton.

Murphey, D., Barry, M., & Vaughn, B. (2015). Adolescent health highlights. *Child Trends,* 1–10.

Nadal, K. L., Griffin, K., Wong, Y., & Rasmus, M. (2014). The impact of racial micro-aggressions on mental health counseling: Implications for clients of color. *Journal of Counseling and Development, 92*(1), 57–66

Nance, J. P. (2015). Dismantling the school-to-prison pipeline: Tools for change. *48 Arizona State Law Journal 313.* Retrieved from https://scholarship.law.ufl.edu/facultypub/767

National Child Traumatic Stress Network. (2008). *Understanding the links between adolescent trauma and substance abuse.* Rockville, MD: Author.

National Commission on Teaching and America's Future. (2007). *The high cost of teacher turnover.* Washington, DC: Author.

National Center for Educational Statistics (NCES). (2016). *The state of racial diversity in the educator workforce.* Washington, DC: Author.

National Institute of Mental Health (2016). *Posttraumatic stress disorder.* Bethesda, MD: Author. Available at: https://www.nimh.nih.gov/health/topics/post-traumatic-stress-disorder-ptsd/index.shtml

National Scientific Center on the Developing Child (2005). Excessive stress disrupts the architecture of the developing brain (Working Paper No. 3). Retrieved from http://www.developingchild.harvard.edu/index.php/resources/reports/resources/reports and working papers/working papers/wp3/

National Scientific Council on the Developing Child (2006). Early exposure to toxic substances damages brain architecture (Working Paper No. 4). Retrieved from http://www.developingchild.harvard.edu/index.php/resources/reports/resources/reports and working papers/working papers/wp4

National Scientific Council on the Developing Child (2007). The timing and quality of early life experiences combine to shape brain architecture (Working Paper No. 5). Retrieved from http://developingchild.harvard.edu/index.php/resources/reports and working papers/working papers/wp5/

National Scientific Council on the Developing Child (2012). The science of neglect: The persistent absence of responsive care disrupts the developing brain (Working Paper No. 12). Retrieved from http://developingchild.harvard.edu/index.php/resources/reports and working papers/working papers/wp12/

Noguera, P. A. (1995). Preventing and producing violence: A critical analysis of responses to school violence. *Harvard Educational Review, 65,* 189–212.

Nystrand, M. (2006). Research on the role of classroom discourse as it affects reading comprehension. *Research in the Teaching of English, 40,* 393–412.

O'Connor, E., & McCartney, K. (2007). Examining teacher child relationships and achievement as part of an ecological model of development. *American Educational Research Journal, 44,* 340–369. doi:10.3102/0002831207302172

Paolucci, E. O., Genuis, M. L., & Violato, C. (2001). A meta-analysis of the published research on the effects of child sexual abuse. *Journal of Psychology, 135,* 17–36.

Parker, P. D., & Martin, A. J. (2009). Coping and buoyancy in the work place: Understanding their effect on teachers' work related well-being and engagement. *Teaching and Teacher Education, 25*(1), 68–75.

Perkins, M., & Graham-Bermann, S. (2012). Violence exposure and the development of school related functioning: Mental health, neurocognition, and learning. *Aggression and Violent Behavior, 17*(1), 89–98.

Perry, B. D. (1997). Incubated in terror: Neurodevelopmental factors in the "cycle of violence." In J. Osofsky (Ed.), *Children, youth and violence* (pp. 124–148). New York, NY: Guilford Press. Retrieved from https://childtrauma.org/wp-content/uploads/2013/11/Incubated_In_Terror.pdf

Perry, B. D. (2006). Applying principles of neurodevelopment to clinical work with maltreated and traumatized children: The neurosequential model of therapeutics. In N. B. Webb (Ed.), *Working with traumatized youth in child welfare* (pp. 27–52). New York, NY: Guilford Press.

Perry, B. D. (2013). *Bonding and attachment in maltreated children: Consequences of emotional neglect in children.* Houston, TX: The Child Trauma Academy.

Perry, B. D. (2014). The cost of caring: Secondary traumatic stress and the impact of working with high risk children and families. Retrieved from https://childtrauma.org/wp-content/uploads/2014/01/Cost_of_Caring_Secondary_Traumatic_Stress_Perry_s.pdf

Pickens, I. B., Siegfried, C. B., Surko, M., & Dierkhising, C. B. (2016). *Victimization and juvenile offending.* Los Angeles, CA: National Child Traumatic Stress Network.

Pietromonaco, P. R., & Barrett, L. F. (2000). The internal working models concept: What do we really know about the self in relation to others? *Review of General Psychology, 4*(2), 155–175.

Pittman, A., Osborn, D. P. J., Rantell, K., & King, M. D. (2016). Bereavement by suicide as a risk factor for suicide attempts. *British Medical Journal Open, 6*(1), e009948. doi: 10.1136/bmjopen-2015-009948

Porche, M. V., Fortuna, L. R., Lin, J., & Alegria, M. (2011). Childhood trauma and psychiatric disorders as correlates of school dropout in a national sample of young adults, *Child Development, 82*(3), 982–998. doi:10.1111/j.1467-8624:20110.01534x

Portnoy, D. (2011, July/August). Burnout and compassion fatigue: Watch for the signs. *Health Progress,* 45–50. Retrieved from http://www.compassionfatigue.org/pages/healthprogress.pdf

Quinn, M., Rutherford, R. B., & Leone, P. F. (2001). *Students with disabilities in correctional facilities.* Reston, VA: ERIC Clearing House on Disabilities and Gifted Education.

Rameson, L. T., & Lieberman, M. (2009). Empathy: A social cognitive neuroscience approach. *Social and Personality Psychology Compass, 3,* 94–110. doi:10.1111/j.1751-9004.2008.00154.x

Roeser, R. W., Skinner, E., Beers, J., & Jennings. P. (2012). Mindfulness training and teachers' professional development. *Child Developmental Perspectives,* 167–173. doi: 10.1111/j.1750-8606.2012.000238.

Romeo, R. D. (2013). The teenage brain: The stress response and the adolescent brain. *Current Directions in Psychological Science, 22*(2), 140–145. doi: 10.1177/0963721413475445.

Ronfeldt, M., Loeb, S., & Wyckoff, J. (2013, February). How teacher turnover harms student achievement. *American Educational Research Journal, 50,* 4–36. doi:10.3102/0002831212463813

Rosenbloom, D. J., Pratt, A. C., & Pearlman. L. A. (1995). Helpers' responses to trauma work: Understanding and intervening in an organization. In B. H. Stamm (Ed.), *Secondary traumatic stress: Self-care issues for clinicians, researchers, and educators* (pp. 65–79). Lutherville, MD: Sidran.

Rudd, T. (2015). *Racial disproportionality in school discipline: Implicit bias is heavily implicated.* Columbus, OH: The Kirwan Institute.

Ruzek, J. I., Brymer, M. J., Jacobs, A. K., Layne, C. M., Vernberg, E. M., & Watson, P. J. (2007). Psychological first aid. *Journal of Mental Health Counseling, 29*(1), 17–49.

Sampson, R. J., Raudenbush, S. W., & Earls, F. (1997). Neighborhoods and violent crime: A multilevel study of collective efficacy. *Science, 15*(277), 918–924. doi: 10.1126/science.277.5328.918

Santa Mina, E. E., & Gallop, R. M. (1998).Childhood sexual and physical abuse and adult self-harm and suicidal behavior: A literature review. *Canadian Journal of Psychiatry, 43*(8), 793–800.

Schneier F. R. (2006) Social anxiety disorder. *The New England Journal of Medicine, 355,* 1029–1036.

Schore, A. N. (1994). *Affect regulation and the origin of the self: The neurobiology of emotional development.* Mahwah, NJ: Lawrence Erlbaum Associates.

Schore, A. N. (2001). Effects of a secure attachment relationship on right brain development, affect regulation, and infant mental health. *Infant Mental Health Journal, 22,* 7–66.

Schore, A. N. (2003). Early relational trauma, disorganized attachment, and the development of a predisposition to violence. In M. Solomon & D. Siegel (Eds.), *Healing trauma: Attachment, mind, body and brain* (pp. 107–167). New York, NY: Norton.

Schore, J., & Schore, A. N. (2008). Modern attachment theory: The central role of affect regulation in development and treatment. *Clinical Social Work Journal, 36,* 9–20. doi:10.1007/s10615-007-0111-7

Schuengel, C., Oosterman, M., & Sterkenburg, P. S. (2009, September 4). Children with disrupted attachment histories: Interventions and psychophysiological indices of effects. *Child and Adolescent Psychiatry and Mental Health, 26.* doi:10.1186/1753-2000-3-26

Schulz, A. J., Zenk, S. N., Israel, B. A., Mentz, G., Stokes, C., & Galea, S. (2008). Do neighborhood economic characteristics, racial composition, and residential stability predict perceptions of stress associated with the physical and social environment? Findings from a multilevel analysis in Detroit. *Journal of Urban Health, 85*(5), 642–661.

Sefa Dei, G. J. (2016). Including the excluded: De-marginalizing immigrant/refugee and racialized students. *Canada Education, 56*(4). Retrieved from http://www.cea-ace.ca/education-canada/article/including-excluded-de-marginalizing-immigrantrefugee-and-racialized-student

Segal, L. (2011). *Culture clash–Immigrant parents and their teens.* Retrieved from http://www.mediate.com/articles/SegalLbl20110425.cfm

Seligman, M. E. P., Steen, T. A., Park, N., & Peterson, C. (2005). Positive psychology progress: Empirical validation of interventions. *American Psychologist, 60,* 410–421.

Shapiro, V. B., Oesterle, S., & Hawkins, J. D. (2015). Relating coalition capacity to the adoption of science-based prevention in communities: Evidence from a randomized trial of communities that care. *American Journal of Community Psychology 5*(1-2*)*, 1–12,

Shepherd, J. (2006). Relations between alcohol, violence and victimization in adolescence. *Journal Adolescence, 29*(4),539–553.

Siegel, D. J. (1999). *The developing mind: Toward a neurobiology of interpersonal experience.* New York, NY: Guilford Press.

Siegel, D.J. (2007). Mindfulness training and neural integration. *Journal of Social, Cognitive, and Affective Neuroscience, 2*(4), 259–263.

Siegel, D. J. (2011). *Mindsight: The new science of personal transformation.* New York, NY: Bantam Books.

Siegel, D. J. (2012). *The developing mind: How relationships and the brain interact to shape who we are* (2nd ed.). New York, NY: Guilford Press.

Siegel, D. J. (2013a). *Brainstorm: The power and purpose of the teenage brain.* New York, NY: Penguin Putnam.

Siegel, D. J. (2013b). Brainstorm: Hyper-rational vs. impulsive behaviors. Retrieved from https://www.youtube.com/watch?v=yqUNtLbwoj4

Siegel, D. J., & Payne Bryson, T. (2012). *The whole-brain child: 12 revolutionary strategies to nurture your child's developing mind.* New York, NY: Bantam.

Simon, S. N., & Johnson, S. M. (2015). Teacher turnover in high-poverty schools: What we know and can do. *Teachers College Record, 117*(3), 1–36.

Simons, R. L., Whitbeck, L. B., Conger, R. D., & Conger, K. J. (1991). Parenting factors, social skills, and value commitments as precursors to school failure, involvement with deviant peers, and delinquent behavior. *Sociology Department, Faculty Publications, 93.* Digital Commons, University of Nebraska–Lincoln.

Singer, M. I., Anglin, T. M., Song, L. Y., & Lunghofe, L. (1995). Adolescents' exposure to violence and associated symptoms of psychological trauma. *Journal of the American Medical Association, 273*(6), 477–482.

Skinner, E., & Beers, J. (2016). Mindfulness and teachers' coping in the classroom: A developmental model of teacher stress, coping, and everyday resilience. In K. Schonert-Reichl & R. W. Roeser (Eds.), *Handbook on mindfulness in education: Emerging theory, research, and programs.* New York, NY: Springer-Verlag.

Smith, C. A., Ireland, T. O., & Thornberry, T. P. (2005). Adolescent maltreatment and its impact on young adult antisocial behavior. *Child Abuse and Neglect, 29,* 1099–1119.

Smith, E. P. (2007). The role of afterschool settings in positive youth development. *Journal of Adolescent Health, 41*(3), 219–220. doi: 10.1016/j.jadohealth.2007.06.010

Smith-Bynum, M. A., Lambert, S. F., English, D., & Ialongo, N. S. (2014). Associations between trajectories of perceived racial discrimination and psychological symptoms among African American adolescents. *Developmental Psychopathology, 26*(401), 1049–1065. doi:10.1017/S0954579414000571

Sood, A., Prasad, K., Schroeder, D., & P. Varkey. (2011). Stress management and resilience training among department of medicine faculty: A pilot randomized clinical trial, *General Internal Medicine, 8,* 858–861. doi: 10, 1007/s11606-011-1640-x

Spann, M. N., Mayes, L. C., Kalmar, J. H., Guiney, J., Womer, F. Y., Pittman, B., Mazure, C. M., Sinha, R., & Blumberg, H. P. (2012). Childhood abuse and neglect and cognitive flexibility in adolescents. *Child Neuropsychology, 18(2)*, 182–189. doi: 10.1080/09297049.2011.595400

Spear, L. (2013). Neurobehavioral changes in adolescents. *Psychological Science, 9*(4), 111–114.

Spillane, J. P., Hallett, T., & Diamond, J. B. (2003). Forms of capital and the construction of leadership: instructional leadership in urban elementary schools. *Sociology of Education, 76*, 1–17.

Sporleder, J., & Forbes, H. T. (2015). *The trauma-informed school: A step-by-step guide for administrators and school personnel.* Boulder, CO: Beyond Consequences, Inc.

Sprague, J. (2014). Integrating PBIS and restorative discipline. *The Special Edge, 27*(3). Retrieved from http://www.calstat.org/publications/article_detail.php?a_id=215&nl_id=130

Squeglia, L. M., Jacobus, B. A., & Tapert, S. F. (2010). The influence of substance use on adolescent brain development. *Clinical EEG Neuroscience, 40*(1), 31–38. doi: 10.1177/1550059404000110

Stapinski, L. A., Bowes, L., Wolke, D., Pearson, R. M., Mahedy, L., Button, K., Lewis, G. , & Araya, R. (2014). Peer victimization during adolescence and risk for anxiety disorders in adulthood: A prospective cohort study. *Depression and Anxiety, 7*, 574–582. doi: 10.1002/da.22270

Steinberg, L. (2007). Risk taking in adolescence: New perspectives from brain and behavior science. *Current Directions in Psychological Science, 16*(2), 55–59.

Steinberg, L. (2014). *Age of opportunity: Lessons from the new science of adolescence.* New York, NY: Houghton Mifflin Harcourt.

Stevens, J. (2012, April 23). Lincoln High School in Walla Walla, WA tries new approach to school discipline–suspensions drop 85%. *ACES Too High News.* Retrieved from https://acestoohigh.com/2012/04/23/lincoln-high-school-in-walla-walla-wa-tries-new-approach-to-school-discipline-expulsions-drop-85/

Stevens, J. (2015). *Adding layers to the ACEs pyramid–What do you think?* Retrieved from http://www.acesconnection.com/search?searching=true&type=0-blogs&queryString=Adding+layers+to+ACEs+pyramid

Sugai, G., Horner, R. H., Dunlap, G., Hieneman, M., Lewis, T. J., Nelson, C. M., & Ruef, M. B. (2000, July). Applying positive behavior support and functional behavioral assessment in schools. *Journal of Positive Behavior Interventions, 2*, 131–143. doi:10.1177/109830070000200302

Synder, H. N. (2005). Juvenile arrests 2003. *OJJDP Juvenile Justice Bulletin*, p. 9.

Tapert, S. F., Aarons, G. A., Sedlar, G. R., & Brown, S. A. (2001). Adolescent substance use and sexual risk-taking behavior. *Journal of Adolescent Health, 28*(3), 181–189.

Tapert, S. F., & Brown, S. A. (1999). Neuropsychological correlates of adolescent substance abuse–four-year outcomes. *Journal of the International Neuropsychological Society, 5*(6), 481–493.

Tedesci, R. G., Park, C. L., & Calhoun, L. G. (1998). *Post traumatic growth: Positive changes in the aftermath of crisis.* New York, NY: Psychology Press.

Teicher, M. H., Anderson, S. L., Polcari, A., Anderson, C. M., & Navalta, C. P. (2002). Developmental neurobiology of childhood stress and trauma. *The Psychiatric Clinics of North America, 25*, 397–426. doi:10.1016/S0193-953X(01)00003-X

Thomas, A., Chess, S., Birch, H. G., Herzig, M. E., & Korn, A. (1963). *Behavioral individuality in early childhood.* New York, NY: New York University Press.

Tomlinson, C. A. (2001). *How to differentiate instruction in mixed-ability classrooms* (2nd ed.). Alexandria, VA: Association for Supervision and Curriculum Development.

Tugade, M. M., Fredrickson, B. L., & Barrett, L. F. (2004). Psychological resilience and positive emotional granularity: Examining the benefits of positive emotions on coping and health. *Journal of Personality, 72,* 1161–1190.

Turner, H. A., Finkelhor, D., & Ormrod, R. (2010). Poly-victimization in a national sample of children and youth. *American Journal of Preventive Medicine, 38*(3), 323–330.

Turner, H. A., Shattuck, A., Finkelhor, D., & Hamby, S. (2016). Poly-victimization and youth violence exposure across contexts. *Adolescent Health, 58*(2), 208–214. doi: http://dx.doi.org/10.1016/j.jadohealth.2015.09.021

U.S. Department of Health and Human Services. (2007). *The Surgeon General's call to action to prevent and reduce underage drinking.* Washington, DC: U.S. Department of Health and Human Services, Office of the Surgeon General.

U.S. Department of Health and Human Services, Administration for Children and Families, Administration on Children, Youth and Families, Children's Bureau. (2016). Child maltreatment 2014. Retrieved from http://www.acf.hhs.gov/programs/cb/research-data-technology/statistics-research/child-maltreatment

U.S. Department of Justice Child Exploitation and Obscenity Section. (2012). *The Administration for Children and Families. Rescue and Restore Campaign tool kits.* Washington, DC: Author.

van der Kolk, B. A. (2001, January). *Remarks at Helping Traumatized Children Learn conference* [Transcript on file at Massachusetts Advocates for Children, 25 Kingston Street, Boston, MA 02111, 617-357-8436]. Paper presented at the Lesley College, Massachusetts Advocates for Children (MAC) and the Task Force on Children Affected by Domestic Violence, Cambridge, MA.

van der Kolk, B. A. (2003). The neurobiology of childhood trauma and abuse. *Child Adolescent Psychiatric Clinics of North America, 12*(2), 293–317.

van der Kolk, B. A. (2005, May). Developmental trauma disorder. *Psychiatric Annals, 35,* 401–408. Retrieved from http://www.wjcia.org/conpast/2008/trauma/trauma.pdf

van der Kolk, B. A. (2014). *The body keeps the score: Brain, mind, and body in the healing of trauma.* New York, NY: Viking.

Vargas, W. M., Bengston, L,, Gilpin, N. W., Whitconb, B. W., & Richardson, H. N. (2014). Alcohol binge drinking during adolescence or dependence during adulthood reduces prefrontal myelin in male rats. *Journal of Neuroscience, 34*(44), 14777–14782. doi:10.1523/JNEUROSCI.3189-13.2014

Vorrath, H., & Brendtro, L. (1985). *Positive peer culture.* Hawthorne, NY: Aldine Publishing.

Vygotsky, L. S. (1986). The genetic roots of thought and speech. In A. Kozulin (Ed. & Trans.), *Thoughts and language* (Rev. ed.). Cambridge, MA: MIT Press.

Wallin, D. J. (2007). *Attachment in psychotherapy.* New York, NY: Guilford Press.

Warren, M. R. (2005). Communities and schools: A new view of urban education reform. *Harvard Educational Review, 75,* 133–173. Retrieved from http://isites.harvard.edu/fs/docs/icb.topic1373484.files/Warren_2005.

Weinberger, D., Elvevag, D., & Giedd, J. (2005). *The adolescent brain: A work in progress.* Washington, DC: The National Campaign to Prevent Teen and Unplanned Pregnancy.

Willis, J. (2007). *Brain friendly strategies for the inclusion classroom.* Alexandria, VA: Association for Supervision and Curriculum Development.

Willis, J. (2011). Three brain-based teaching strategies to build executive function in students. Retrieved from https://www.edutopia.org/topics

Wilson, J. Q., & Kelling, G. L. (1982, March 1). Broken windows: The police and neighborhood safety. *The Atlantic, 249,* 29–38. Retrieved from http://www.theatlantic.com/magazine/archive/1982/03/broken-windows/304465/

Wolinsky, F. D., & Johnson, R. J. (1991). The use of health services by older adults. *Journal of Gerontology, 46,* 345–357.

Wolpow, R., Johnson, M. M., Hertel, R., & Kincaid, S. O. (2009). *The heart of learning and teaching: Compassion, resiliency, and academic success.* Retrieved from http://www.k12.wa.us/compassionateschools/pubdocs/theheartoflearningandteaching.pdf

Wolfe, P. (2010). *Brain matters: Translating research into classroom practice.* Reston, VA: Association for Supervision and Curriculum Development.

Wordes, M., & Nunez, M. L. (2002). *Our vulnerable teenagers: Their victimization, its consequences, and directions for prevention and intervention.* Washington, DC: National Council on Crime and Delinquency.

Worsley, L. (2007). *The resilience doughnut model: A model showing the interaction of external resources that build individual resilience.* Retrieved from https://www.resiliencereport.com/var/file/research/The%20resilience%20doughnut%20general%20paper.pdf

Zapf, D. (2002). Emotion work and psychological well-being: A review of the literature and some conceptual considerations. *Human Resource Management Review, 12,* 237–268. doi: 10.1016/S1053-4822(02)00048-7

Zeigler, D. W., Wang, C. C., Yoast, R. A., Dickinson, B. D., McCaffree, M.A., Robinowitz, C. B., & Sterling, M. L. (2005). The neurocognitive effects of alcohol on adolescents and college students. *Preventive Medicine, 40*(1), 23–32.

Zullig, K., Huebner, E., & Patton, J. (2011). Relationships among school climate domains and school satisfaction: Further validation of the school climate measure. *Psychology in the Schools, 48,* 133–145. doi: 10.1002/pits.20532

# Index

# About the Author

*Susan E. Craig*, PhD, is a lifelong student of early trauma and its effects on children's learning. Her teaching experience, as well as years of onsite training and technical assistance to school districts throughout the country, provides the context for her advocacy for trauma-sensitive educational reform.

Dr. Craig began her writing career in 1992 with an article in *Phi Delta Kappan* describing the educational needs of children living with violence. This work received special notice in the now-famous "purple book" *Helping Traumatized Children Learn*, published by Massachusetts Advocates for Children: Trauma and Policy Initiative. Her texts *Reaching and Teaching Children Who Hurt: Strategies for Your Classroom* (2008) and *Trauma-Sensitive Schools: Learning Communities Transforming Children's Lives, K–5* (2016) are best-sellers among teachers and administrators who use them to guide their efforts to make schools more accessible to students with early trauma histories. In 2013, Dr. Craig was among those interviewed in the Safe Start National Resource Center series profiling women who have made an impact on the issue of children's exposure to violence.

Dr. Craig is an avid blogger and sought-after public speaker. In 2014, she participated in the Attachment and Trauma Network's Educating Traumatized Children Summit. Her blog www.meltdownstomastery.wordpress.com is read by educators from around the world.